Louis Icart

The Complete Etchings

Fig. 1. Summer Dreams, *Vacances*, 1934, 19⅝
x 17⅝, ul-16★

Louis Icart
The Complete Etchings

William R. Holland
Clifford P. Catania
Nathan D. Isen

With participation of Myles Phillip Burton and Richard Perozzi

Schiffer Publishing Ltd

1469 Morstein Road, West Chester, Pennsylvania 19380

Published by Schiffer Publishing, Ltd.
1469 Morstein Road
West Chester, Pennsylania 19380
Please write for a free catalog
This book may be purchased from the publisher.
Please include $2.00 postage.
Try your bookstore first.

Printed in the United States of America.
ISBN: 0-88740-254-2

See Appendix I: Title Cross Reference for other titles by which an asterisked etching is known.

Contents

Louis Icart

Acknowledgements

A book of this magnitude could not possibly have been completed without much assistance. Our fondest thanks and appreciation go out to all who have had confidence in our project and the patience to endure the inconvenience we may have caused them. We have endeavored to include all who have helped us throughout our long journey. It is our sincere hope that no one has been overlooked.

We must first acknowledge the great contribution of Myles Phillip Burton and Richard Perozzi. Their love of Louis Icart dates back more than two decades years before Icart's resurgent popularity. Through diligent and deliberate searching in this country and Europe, they have amassed an impressive collection covering Icart's entire artistic career, with a special emphasis on early and rare pieces. Their recognition of the inherent beauty of Icart allowed them to acquire many choice pieces before the deluge of competing collectors entered the field.

In addition, Myles has done much research into accurate titling and dating Icart's etchings. Although this may cause some confusion with previously accepted titles, we feel the proper titles should now be used. We have included a title cross-reference to minimize confusion.

We wish to thank the following colleagues and collectors who allowed us to photograph their etchings: Sam Samuelian a patient friend; Carol Haley; Phil Burch; Christies, especially Peggy Gilges; Phil Chasen; Michael Kam; Adrienne Leff; Bruce Marine; Larry Klepper; Jane Moufflet; Lynne Stark; Dottie and John Freeman; Alan Teal; Kazumi Arikawa; Daphne & David Peggs; and a special thanks to Philip "Flip" Rosenfeld and Alan Schleifer.

We also appreciate the patience of Peter Schiffer, who kept faith even after we twice missed our deadline. We salute Darrel Hookway for his diligence in procuring etchings for the book, and Steve DeBottis for reframing countless pictures without complaint.

Fig. 2. Youth, *Jeunesse*, 1930, 23⅞ x 15⅜,
ul-15a

Fig. 3. Mardi Gras, *A La Fête*, 1936, 18⅝ x
18¼, ul-16

Introduction

In assembling this book we dedicated ourselves to compiling the most comprehensive work on the etchings of Louis Icart. This presented a challenge since his career spanned forty years and yielded hundreds of works on copper. Our efforts have added well over one hundred etchings to the number which were previously documented. The majority of these most recently discovered etchings date from Icart's Fashion Period of 1910-1914. After completing several years of exhaustive work, we are satisfied that the majority of gaps in the record of Icart's career is now filled.

Much has already been written about Louis Icart's life by S. Michael Schnessel in his several excellent books. We applaud that author's diligence and determination in building a sturdy foundation of scholarly interest in this field. We decided not to duplicate his extensive background material. Rather, we chose to preserve space for the presentation of Icart's etchings in a larger format. Another high priority was to showcase as many etchings as possible in full color since this evokes a more realistic mood from the works. We meticulously recorded precise size measurements and included printed copyright notations for all etchings in a special index. Etchings that were originally marketed as decorative sets are shown together in this book. And finally, works marked with an asterisk have alternate titles that are listed in an alphabetical cross-reference at the rear of the book.

This book presents the whole chronology of Icart's work in copper plate engraving on a year-by-year basis. It is like a sumptuous feast of remarkable impact and diversity. In summation, there appears to be one ultimate drive behind all that Louis Icart created: an absorbing desire to bring beauty and pleasure to viewers for generation after generation.

Fig. 4. Wing Chair, c.1914, 20¾ x 16¾, no
copyright information

Chapter One
Fashion Period

1911-1915

Louis Icart was fortunate to begin his artistic career in Paris at a time when artists from both traditional and progressive movements commingled in an energized atmosphere of creativity. He could observe an entire spectrum of styles and a wide variety of techniques employed in various media. Unlike today, copper plate engraving and etching were still important methods of expression explored by most artists. When our blossoming artist tried his hand at these techniques in copper, he quickly discovered that he possessed a special talent for creating desirable etchings. With most of his early employment centered on illustrating clothing lines for French fashion houses, it is not surprising that his earliest works on copper were fashion oriented in appearance.

The Fashion Period, as we call it, began about 1910, although it is difficult to assign an exact date due to the lack of notations on most early works. Once inspired, Icart clearly forged ahead by creating dozens of similarly styled works in the years before World War I. Each work was hand-signed in pencil in the lower right margin. The signature found on these early engravings is more spontaneous and scrawled than that seen in later years.

Edition sizes, the total number of etchings produced per plate, were kept small as Icart struggled to establish his reputation. In general, pencil notations in the lower left margin indicate that between 25 and 100 works were printed before the plate was destroyed. Consequently, these works are extremely difficult to locate today. The lack of any catalogues or inventory lists from the Fashion years makes reconstruction of Icart's total output a slow, tedious process. The occasional printer who obtained a copyright for one of these early etchings and then printed a notation in the margin, has helped us to reconstruct this most difficult period. The fact that Icart used several different printing firms in an on-and-off way, makes the jig-saw puzzle just a bit more complex.

Fig. 5. Vanity, 1911, 15 x 7½, ur-3b

Fig. 6. Robert Arnot (Printed Logo)

Fig. 7. Before the Stroll, 1911, 15 x 11⅛, lc-1

Fig. 8. Cercle Librairie Estampes (Embossed Seal)

By strict definition, Icart's fashion pieces are engravings in that they were created largely through the carving of simple lines of varying thickness and depth into the copper's surface. Icart would not "etch" his plates with acids until later phases of his career. Since Fashion pieces are engravings, they appear more linear and dependent upon an object's basic form than works from future decades. Although Icart's techniques would still broaden and mature further, the greatest accomplishment was achieved during these earliest years of the decade. He mastered the ability to regularly draw charming, youthful faces that would become the foundation for all his etchings thereafter.

Fig. 9. Pink Rose, 1911, 23⅝ x 12¼, cl-1

Fig. 10. Edmee, *Edmée,* c.1913, 13¼ x 4⅞, no
copyright information

Fig. 11. Swimsuit, c.1913, 11¼ x 7⅞, no
copyright information

Fig. 12. Dress Shop, c.1913, 6⅜ x 7⅝, no
copyright information

Fig. 13. Cat, *Le Chat*, 1913, 11¼ x 7¼, ul-3

Fig. 14. Mouse, *Le Souris*, 1913, 11½ x 7¾, ul-3

Fig. 15. Shopping, c.1914, 14 x 6½, no copyright information

Fig. 18. Elegance, c.1913, 15½ x 9¾, no copyright information

Fig. 16. Tasseled Purse, c.1914, 14¼ x 5½, no copyright information

Fig. 17. Windy Day, c.1913, 10⅝ x 7⅜, no copyright information .

During the Fashion Period, the Icart girl was usually drawn against a nearly vacant background. Only a few brief lines of shading were added behind the model to imply a three-dimensional world. The intention was to spotlight the central figure without distraction from unnecessary objects. The rare inclusion of pets or furniture was employed merely for props to help position or emphasize the lady. The observer is required to focus his attention on the beauty and implications that surround the woman alone. To successfully present such an easy, natural beauty through such a simple format is the crowning achievement of Icart's early work.

We enjoy the Fashion Period for its clean, young innocence. Watching the conception of ideas and the birth of newfound abilities gives us satisfaction in knowing that these gifts will bless Icart through the remainder of his career. Perhaps we pursue Icart's early Fashion works with a fervor equal to our own nostalgic quests for things from our youths. As we see the dawning of that adorable Icart girl's face, it as if we are looking upon something newborn, pure, and full of promise.

15

Fig. 20. Cupid Bellboy, c.1913, 14¾ x 10, no copyright information

Fig. 19. Empire Dress, c.1911, 18¼ x 9½, no copyright information

Fig. 21. Conversation, c.1914, size unknown, no copyright information

Fig. 22. Mysterious Guest, c.1914, 12 x 4, no
copyright information

Fig. 24. First Pet, c.1914, 19¼ x 14, no
copyright information

Fig. 23. Fur Stole, c.1914, size unknown, no
copyright information

Fig. 25. Modesty, c.1914, 10⅞ x 8⅞, no copyright information

Fig. 26. Curious, c.1914, 9 x 12⅛, no copyright information

Fig. 27. Suggling, c.1914, 10⅝ x 13, lr-a

Fig. 29. Little Dog, *Petit Chien*, 1914, 11½ x 7½, ul-b

Fig. 28. Bouquet, *Bouquet*, 1914, 20⅛ x 10¾, ul-b

Fig. 30. At The Opera I, c.1914, 20⅝ x 14¼,
no copyright information

Fig. 31. At the Opera II, c.1914, 20⅜ x 14, no
copyright information

Fig. 33. Tango Dancers I, c.1914, size
unknown, no copyright information

Fig. 32. Tango Dancers II, c.1914, size
unknown, no copyright information

Fig. 34. Coursing I, *Coursing*, c.1914, 11¾ x
16⅜, no copyright information

Fig. 35. Praise, c.1914, 19⅛ x 15⅜, no
copyright information

Fig. 36. Playmates, c.1914, 10 x 6¾, no
copyright information

Fig. 38. Dream, *La Rêve*, c.1914, 8⅜ x 11⅝, no copyright information

Fig. 39. Safe Keeping, c.1914, 15⅛ x 7¾, no copyright information

Fig. 40. Fireplace, c.1914, 12 x 9, no copyright information

Fig. 41. Divan, *Le Divan*, c.1914, size unknown, no copyright information

Fig. 42. Tete-a-Tete, c.1914, 10¾ x 13½, no copyright information

Fig. 43. Reverie, *Reverie*, c.1914, 11⅛ x 10⅞, no copyright information

Fig. 44. Garter, c.1914, 11¼ x 7⅛, no
copyright information

Fig. 46. Wading, c1914, 14⅞ x 9⅞, no
copyright information

Fig. 45. Gathering Apples, c.1914, 13⅜ x 5⅛,
no copyright information

Fig. 48. First Beautiful Days, *Premiers Beaus Jours*, c.1914, 9¼ x 15⅛, no copyright information

Fig. 47. Springtime Vision, *Vision Printanière*, c.1914, 11¼ x 18⅝, no copyright information

Fig. 48. First Beautiful Days, *Premiers Beaus Jours*, c.1914, 9¼ x 15⅛, no copyright information

Fig. 49. Butterfly, *Le Papillon*, c.1914, 11 x 19, no copyright information

Fig. 50. Unexpected Guest, c.1914, 16⅝ x
9⅞, no copyright information

Fig. 51. Muff, *Le Manchon*, 1914, 20¼ x 11,
ul-b

Fig. 52. Hat Box, c.1914, 13⅝ x 10½, no
copyright information

Fig. 53. Flirtation, c.1914, 13¼ x 10⅝, no
copyright information

Fig. 55. Golf, *Le Golf*, c.1914, 17⅛ x 11¼, no
copyright information

Fig. 54. Rosebud, 1914, 11¾ x 7¾, ul-b

Fig. 56. Tickling, c. 1914, 16 x 11½, no copyright information

Fig. 57. Blue Sash, 1914, 14 x 16, ul-3b

Fig. 58. Careless, *Petit Accident*, c. 1914, 11⅞ x 6⅛, ul-2

Fig. 59. Masquerade, c.1915, 12 x 7⅜, ul-2

Fig. 59a. Cat Caress, c.1914, 15¾ x7¾, no
copyright information

Fig. 59b. Tender Grapes, c.1914, 16⅝ x 11½,
no copyright information

Fig. 59e. Enticement, c.1914, 13⅝ x 11¼, lr-a

Fig. 59d. Snowy Night, c.1914, 9⅛ x 7½, no copyright information

Fig. 59f. At the Ball, c.1914, size unknown, no copyright information

Fig. 60. Winged Victory, *L'as Vainquer,*
c.1918, 21¼ x 14⅞, no copyright information

Chapter Two

War Period

1917-1918

During World War I, Louis Icart served France in the Infantry and later as a pilot in the Air Corps. He had a firsthand opportunity to appraise the sad mix of courage, patriotism, and horror associated with such a cataclysm. As an artist, he was compelled to represent what he saw through his work. Unfortunately, his responsibilities as a soldier limited the total number of etchings he could produce during these war years.

Icart began to experiment by printing the same plate on different types of paper. We find works printed on both the thin, waxy Japon paper, as well as the heavier Arches and Van Gelder papers. Pencil notations of edition size are usually found in the lower left-hand margin. Pieces were usually printed with an edition of 25 works on Japon paper, while 75 to 150 sheets of a heavier paper were run from the plate as well. Including all the types of paper used, the total edition size would equal 100 to 175 works.

War etchings never bear any impressed seals or printed logos from either a printer or Icart himself. Similarly, they have no copyright notations to aid us in giving them exact dates. All pieces do bear the artist's pencil signature in the lower right-hand margin. Again, it is the "early signature"; more open and free-flowing than that we commonly associate with later works. Some of Icart's war etchings strike collectors as a bit traditional or predictable. However, it is most likely the somber mood of war reflected in these works that encourages such a viewpoint. For these pieces must be taken in the context of the patriotic emotions they strove to evoke. They were highly symbolic; meant to represent the combined will of the people to staunchly preserve their liberty. Therefore, we might expect these etchings to depict determined, unyielding soldiers, or classically-dressed women bearing the standards of Allied nations. Icart purposely composed them to be solid and statuesque in both feeling and appearance.

Icart's technical ability in engraving the war

Fig. 61. Angry Steed, *Le Coursier en Colère*, c.1917, 15⅝ x 9⅝, no copyright information

Fig. 61A. Icart's Early Signature (c.1911-c.1925)

Fig. 62. After the Raid, c.1917, 15⅛ x 19⅞,
no copyright information

Fig. 63. Defense of the Homeland, *Défense du
Foyer, c.1917, 15¼ x 21¾, no copyright
information* ⋆

36

Fig. 64. Human Grenade, *La Grenade,* c. 1917, 17⅜ x 12, no copyright information ★

Fig. 65. Inquest, c.1917, 15⅛ x 19⅛, no copyright information

Fig. 66. Bird of Prey, c.1918, 18¼ x 12¾, no copyright information

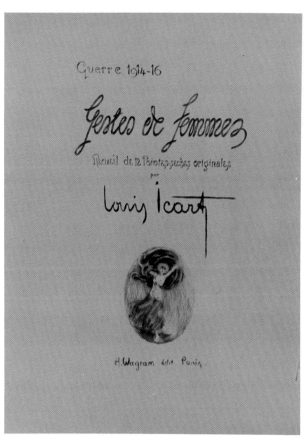

Fig. 67. Chronicles of Women (Title Page), c.1917, size unknown, no copyright information

Fig. 68. Chronicles of Women (The Replacement), *Celle Qui Remplace*, c.1917, 6⅞ x 10, no copyright information

Fig. 69. Chronicles of Women (The Godmother) with remarque, *La Mariane*, c.1917, 6⅞ x 10, no copyright information

Fig. 70. Chronicles of Women (The Prisoner), c.1917, 6⅞ x 10, no copyright information

Fig. 71. Chronicles of Women (Those Who Flee), *Celles Qui Fuient*, c.1917, 6⅞ x 10, no copyright information

Fig. 72. Chronicles of Women (She Who Hopes) with remarque, *Celle Qui Espere*, c.1917, 6⅞ x 10, no copyright information

Fig. 73. Chronicles of Women (Those Who Cry) with remarque, *Celles Qui Pleurent*, c.1917, 6⅞ x 10, no copyright information

Fig. 74. Chronicles of Women (The Strategist), *La Stratege*, c.1917, 6⅞ x 10, no copyright information

Fig. 75. Chronicles of Women (The Supplier), c.1917, 6⅞ x 10, no copyright information

Fig. 77. Chronicles of Women (She Who Works), *Celle Qui Travaille,* c. 1917, 6⅞ x 10, no copyright informaion ★

Fig. 78. Chronicles of Women (She Who Cultivates), *Celle Qui Pioche,* c. 1917, 6⅞ x 10, no copyright information

Fig. 76. Chronicles of Women (The Wife), *L'Espouse, c.1917, 6⅞ x 10, no copyright information*

Fig. 79. Chronicles of Women (Nurse) with remarque, *L'Infirmiere,* c.1917, 6⅞ x 10, no copyright information

Fig. 80. In the Trenches, *Dans Les Tranchées*,
c.1917, 11½ x 18¾,no copyright information

Fig. 81. Voice of the Cannon, *La Voix du Canon*, c.1917, 15⅞ x 23, no copyright
information

pieces is superb. Their beauty far outweighs the importance of the severity of their mood. His models are excellently drawn and posed. They begin to take on weight and substance. Icart begins to develop more realistic settings that clearly reassure the observer that the events depicted are occurring in real time and space. And in several works, the artist employs technical devices that imply movement and inherent energy to people and objects. Things are bursting, tumbling, flying and surging forth.

By far, the most popular etchings produced during the War are those that first offer a glimpse into Icart's fruitful imagination. Take for example the spectacle of the personification of Liberty as a woman exploding forth from the muzzle of a cannon. And even more satisfying, the hovering flight of a lady whose robe becomes wings amidst a raging dogfight of biplanes. Icart has realized his ability to excite the audience through powerful visual imagery.

Fig. 82. Kiss of the Motherland, *La Baiser de la Mère Patrie*, c.1917, 19¼ x 11½, no copyright information ★

Fig. 83. Courage, My Legions, c.1917, 21⅜ x 16½, no copyright information

Fig. 84. Flame, c.1917, 19¾ x 16¾, no copyright information

Fig. 85. Miss Liberty, c.1917, 19¼ x 12⅝, no copyright information

Perhaps more than in any other phase of his career, in the War Period Louis Icart allows his personal feelings to show through his etchings. His presentation clearly warns us of the stark savagery and futility of war. This point is even more profound when we realize just how thoroughly World War I was able to distract the attention of a man normally focused on pleasure and beauty. And yet, once it was over, Icart shared the desire of the world to look ahead and enjoy the freedoms that were won. The challenge to live daringly and joyously was at hand.

Fig. 86. Victory Wreath, c.1917, 20¼ x 16¼,
no copyright information ★

Fig. 87. Homage to Guynemere, c.1917, 19¼
x 15⅜, no copyright information ★

Fig. 88. Marianne, *La Marseillaise*, c.1918,
19¼ x 11⅞, no copyright information ⋆

Fig. 90. Nurse, c.1917, 19⅜ x 15⅜, no
copyright information

Fig. 89. Britannia, c.1918, 19⅜ x 11⅜, no
copyright information ⋆

Fig. 91. Favorite Scent, c.1920, 14 x 9¼, no
copyright information

Chapter Three
Early Twenties

1919-1924

Immediately after World War I, Louis Icart once again began to create etchings that depicted beautiful, carefree women in their seductive misadventures. Trends in society were leaning towards greater sexual permissiveness both in fashion and behavior itself. Icart's deliciously naughty works were particularly well-poised to tap into a large and eager market. While the artist continued to perfect his technical abilities, he also used these years to meter and gauge the exact desires of the public towards household art. He used this period to develop business contacts and marketing techniques that would later prove fantastically successful.

Etchings from the Early Twenties were still produced in small editions ranging from 50-300 pieces per plate. Actual edition notations were often penciled onto the lower left margins of each sheet. Naturally with each year of growing success, the edition sizes were increased. Sometime around 1923 or 1924, Icart abandoned the practice of annotating each etching with its production sequence number. Though the exact reason for this is unknown, it is assumed that Icart started basing edition size on the market demand for each work, rather than preplanning a specific edition size at the outset of printing. As a result, he could not foretell the total number he would ultimately run from any given plate. The majority of Icart etchings produced in the early Twenties were copyrighted through the F. H. Bresler & Co. of Milwaukee, which we believe had some agreement with the artist for distribution in the United States. Most of these works were also copyrighted by the Estampe Moderne, a fine art distributor based in Paris. The firm's impressed "EM" seal is often found pressed into the lower margin paper about one to two inches below the image. When both Icart and his distributing companies neglected to obtain copyrights, those etchings come to us without dates to set them in proper chronology. In such instances, we are left to rely on the stylistic features of the works to

Fig. 92. Chinese Mask, *Masque Chinois*, c.1919, 14⅝ x 10⅞, no copyright information

Fig. 93. Estampe Moderne (Embossed Seal)

Fig. 94. Under the Apple Tree, c.1919, 11¼
x 18⅝, no copyright information

Fig. 95. Gavotte, *La Gavotte*, c.1919, 21½ x
16⅜, no copyright information ★

estimate their date. In general, etchings created
during the Early Twenties period still carry the
earlier Icart signature described in previous
sections.

During this time, Icart first became fascinated
with exploiting specific themes in a series of
related etchings. This is most apparent in his
frequent representations of the Four Seasons. In
such a set, four works can be joined through both
composition and idea to follow a group of lovely
ladies through the changes of the year. We have
discovered six sets of seasons in Icart's work.
When enthused by anything he deemed worthy,
the artist manipulated that object through a
series of etchings in a variety of situations. We
have such categories as monkeys, parrots, satyrs,
cherubs, birds, buddhas, goldfish, fruit trees,
flowers, baskets, jugs, and masks! Often, Icart
conceived two works of similar size and subject
matter as a "pair," and marketed them as such.
They could be displayed in balance on either side
of a doorway or mantel. This relationship of pairs
remains important throughout the entire decade
of the Twenties.

Fig. 96. Beauty Mark, c.1919, 10¼ x 7¼, no
copyright information

Fig. 97. Rouging, c.1919, 10¼ x 7¼, no
copyright information

As she entered the Twenties, the Icart Girl no longer had to fend for herself in a sparse drypoint world. The artist enthusiastically experimented with a multitude of techniques in the aquatint method. This involves using acid baths to burn selected parts of the copper's surface to create varied textures. The results more realistically approximate a three-dimensional world through areas of shadow and light. The varied patterns and tones in both gentle and abrupt gradations would be unobtainable through the use of drypoint alone. This use of aquatint methods became an integral part of Icart's etchings from this point onward in his career. The unique patterns were routinely incorporated thereafter into creating the visual effect of skies, fields, buildings, garments, and floor designs. The resultant combination of the standard drypoint with the newfound freedom of aquatint added a fullness to the visual effect of the works. They were more interesting and more nearly realistic.

Fig. 98. Spring (Again), *Printemps*, c.1919, 10½ x 7⅜, no copyright information

Fig. 99. Summer (Breeze), *L'Eté*, c.1919, 7⅜ x 10⅝, no copyright information

As the Twenties established itself as being a decade of bold fun and experimentation, Icart began to permit longer glimpses of a more liberated woman. She is no longer a lady caught off guard in an accident, but rather one who is curious and willing to experiment. She is sensual, seductive, and carefree. She lounges in alluring gowns, rests on plush couches, surrounds herself with things most vivid and exotic. She dances, smokes, and plays with evident passion. And she is no longer shy about inviting us up to her room. The "bedroom etching" is born; for that is where we can now go with her.

What is clear from this period is the rapid advance that Louis Icart made in creativity, composition, and technique. Through these six years his women were given a much better world in which to exist, a place more colorful, detailed, and unrestricted. It was now a personal world where one could play, hide, contemplate, and romance. It is so much like our own that it demands we step back a bit to find it hidden right under our noses, passing in the sparkling eyes of some beautiful woman.

Fig. 100. Autumn (Storm), *Automne*, c.1919, 10½ x 7⅜, no copyright information

Fig. 101. Winter (Warmth), *L'Hiver*, c.1919, 7⅜ x 10½, no copyright information

Fig. 102. Mother & Child, c.1919, 15⅜ x 9⅜, no copyright information

Fig. 103. Incident, *Un Incident*, 1920, 8¼ x 10⅜, ul-3a

Fig. 104. Scared, 1920, 11 x 14⅞, ur-4, ul-c ★

Fig. 105. Bewilderment, *L'Ahurissement*, 1920,
18⅛ x 15, ur-4, ul-c

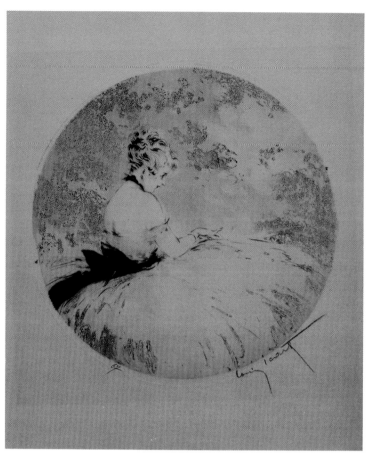

Fig. 106. Spring (In Pink), *Printemps*, 1920, 8⅝ diameter, ur-4, ul-c

Fig. 107. Summer (In Yellow), *L'Eté*, 1920, 8⅝ diameter, ur-4, ul-c

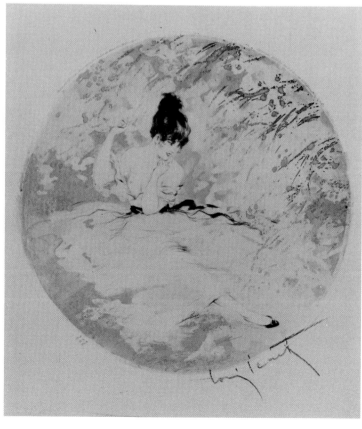

Fig. 108. Autumn (In Purple), *Automne*, 1920, 8⅝ diameter, ur-4, ul-c

Fig. 109. Winter (In Blue), *L'Hiver*, 1920, 8¾ diameter, ur-4, ul-c

Fig. 111. Favorite, 1920, 19¼ x 14¾, no
copyright information

Fig. 110. String of Beads, 1920, 17 x 12, ur-4,
ul-c

Fig. 112. Roses, *Les Roses*, c.1920, 14⅛ x 17⅞,
no copyright information

Fig. 113. Prelude, c.1920, 14½ x 20⅝, no
copyright information

Fig. 114. Grapes, 1920, 15⅝ x 10⅞, lr-c, ll-4

Fig. 115. Black Bows, 1920, 16⅜ x 11¼, lr-c, ll-4

Fig. 116. Afternoon of a Faun, *L'après-midi d'un Faune*, c.1920, 10½ x 13¼, no copyright information

Fig. 117. Frolicking, 1920, 14¼ x 18¾, ur-4, ul-c

Fig. 118. Blue Macaw, 1920, 18½ x 15¼, ur-4,
ul-c

Fig. 119. Spring (Buds), *Printemps*, 1920, 9½ x
7⅜, ur-4, ul-c

Fig. 120. Summer (Parasol), *L'Eté*, 1920,
9½ x 7⅜, ur-4, ul-c

Fig. 121. Autumn (Plums), *Automne*, 1920, 9½ x 7⅜, ur-4, ul-c

Fig. 122. Winter (Snowflakes), 1920, 9½ x 7⅜, ur-4, ul-c

Fig. 125. Green Parakeets, 1920, 17⅛ x 12¼, ur-4, ul-c

Fig. 126. Indiscreet Cockatoo, *Le Cacatoès Indiscret*, 1921, 13¼ x 10⅝, ur-4, ul-c

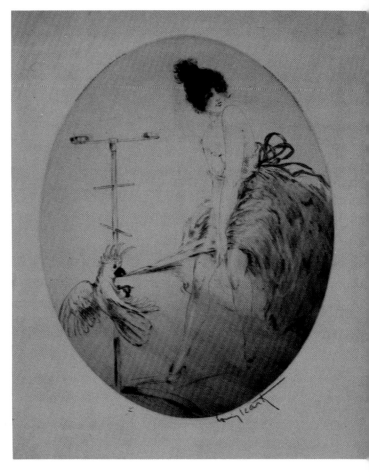

Fig. 123. Carnival, *Au Carnival*, 1920, 14¾ x 18¼, ur-4, ul-c

Fig. 124. Seduction, *Le Faune*, 1921, 14⅜ x 19, ur-4, ul-c

Fig. 127. Lou Lou, 1921, 16⅞ x 11⅞, ur-4, ul-c

Fig. 128. Plate of Milk, 1921, 15 x 11¼, ur-4, ul-d

Fig. 129. Venetian Shawl, *Le Châle Vénitien*,
1921, 14⅛ x 8⅛, ur-4, ul-d ★

Fig. 130. Lacquered Screen, *Le Paravent de
Laque*, 1922, 14 x 8¼, ur-4a, ul-d

Fig. 131. Puppet Show, 1921, 14⅜ x 19⅛, ur-4, ul-c

Fig. 132. Puppets, *Marionnettes*, 1922, 14½ x 19⅛, ur-4, ul-d

Fig. 133. Spilled Oranges, *Les Oranges Renversées*, 1921, 15⅛ x 11⅛, ur-4, ul-d

Fig. 134. Sleeping Cat, *Le Chat Qui Dort*, c.1922, 11¼ x 10⅝, no copyright information

Fig. 135. Before Christmas, *Les Colis*, c.1922,
14½ x 9⅝, ul-11

Fig. 136. Christmas Wreath, c.1922, 14¾ x 9⅞, ul-11

Fig. 137. Doves, *Les Colombes*, 1922, 14 x 13½, ur-4a, ul-d

Fig. 138. Patience, 1922, 7⅜ x 9⅜, ur-4a, ul-e

Fig. 139. Contentment, 1922, 7⅜ x 9⅜, ur-4a,
ul-e

70

Fig. 140. Spanish Comb, 1922, 17½ x 14⅛, ur-4a, ul-d ★

Fig. 141. Spanish Shawl, *Le Châle Espagnole*, 1922, 15¾ x 12⅞,

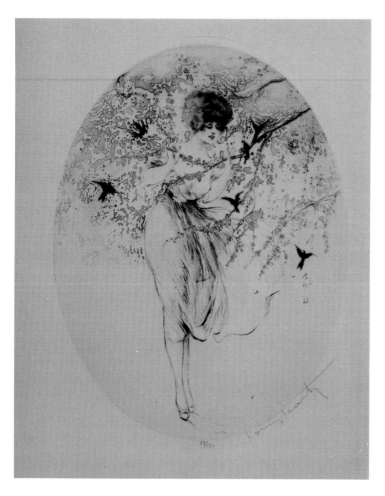

Fig. 142. Spring (Blackbirds), *Printemps*, c.1922, 9⅜ x 7¼, no copyright information

Fig. 143. Summer (Fruit), *L'Eté*, c.1922, 9⅜ x 7¼, no copyright information

Fig. 144. Autumn (Bonnet), *Automne*, c.1922, 9⅜ x 7¼, no copyright information

Fig. 145. Winter (Chestnuts), *L'Hiver*, c.1922, 9⅜ x 7¼, no copyright information

Fig. 146. Untied Ribbon, *Le Ruban Denoue*,
1922, 18¼ x 13¼, ul-d, ur-4a

Fig. 147. Playfulness, *Joueuse*, c.1922, 17 x 12,
no copyright information

Fig. 148. Tsar, 1922, 9⅜ x 7⅝, ur-4a, ul-e

Fig. 149. Vola, 1922, 9⅜ x 7⅝, ur-4a, ul-e

Fig. 151. Broken Blue Jug, 1922, 17⅝ x 12⅝, ur-4a, ul-d ★

Fig. 150. Empty Cage, *La Cage Vide*, 1922, 17⅝ x 12¾, ur-4a, ul-d ★

Fig. 152. In the Nest, 1922, 19 x 11¼, ur-4a, ul-d

Fig. 153. On the Branches, 1922, 19 x 11¼, ur-4b, ul-d ★

Fig. 154. Do Not Enter, *On N'Entre Pas*,
1922, 16¾ x 10¼, ur-4a, ul-d

Fig. 155. New Grapes, 1922, 19¼ x 13, ur-4a,
ul-d ★

Fig. 156. Behind the Fan, *L'Eventail*, 1922,
14¾ x 19⅛, ur-4a, ul-d

Fig. 157. Weary, *Fatique*, 1922, 13½ x 20, ur-
4a, ul-d

Fig. 158. Blindfold, *Le Bandeau*, 1922, 14¼ x
17½, ur-4, ul-e

Fig. 159. Clipped Wings, c.1922, 15⅜ x 11⅜,
ur-7, ul-h

Fig. 160. Snow, 1922, 19½ x 14¼, ur-4a, ul-d

Fig. 161. Puff of Smoke, 1922, 19¼ x 13⅝, ur-4b, ul-d

Fig. 162. Love Birds, 1922, 18¼ x 13¼, ur-4a, ul-d

Fig. 163. Blue Butterflies, 1922, 19½ x 14, ur-4a, ul-d

Fig. 164. Autumn Chill, c.1923, 12½ x 16⅜, no copyright information

Fig. 165. Reine, c.1923, size unknown, no copyright information

Fig. 166, Tou Tou, *Mon Tou Tou*, 1923, 14 x
10¼, ur-9, ul-h

Fig. 167. Minouche, *Minouche*, 1923, 14 x 10¼,
ur-9, ul-h

Fig. 168. Fanny, c.1923, 15⅜ x 10⅝, no copyright information

Fig. 170. At the Urn, c.1923, 12⅞ x 17⅛, ur-7, ul-h

Fig. 171. Peacock Shawl, 1923, 12¾ x 16¾, ur-9, ul-11

Fig. 169. Black Hat, c.1923, 12⅝ x 11¼, no copyright information *

84

Fig. 172. Blue Bonnet, *Le Bonnet Bleu*, 1923, 17½ x 12⅞, ur-9, ul-h

Fig. 173. Letter, *Le Lettre*, 1923, 17½ x 12⅝, ur-9, ul-h

Fig. 174. Feathered Shawl, c.1923, 14¼ x 11½, no copyright information

Fig. 175. Lemon Tree, c.1923, 17⅜ x 11½, ur-7, ul-h

Fig. 176. Spring (Apples), *Printemps*, c.1923,
10½ x 7½, no copyright information

Fig. 178. Autumn (Grapes), *Automne*, c. 1923,
10½ x 7½, no copyright information

Fig. 177. Summer (Oranges), *L'Eté*, c.1923,
10½ x 7½, no copyright information

Fig. 179. Winter (Snowtree), *L'Hiver*, c.1923,
10½ x 7½, no copyright information

Fig. 180. Kittens, *Petits Chats*, c.1923, 14⅛ x
18¾, ur-7, ul-h

Fig. 181. Fishing, 1923, 14⅛ x 18¾, ur-9, ul-h

Fig. 182. Best Friends, c.1923, 16⅜ x 13⅜, ur-7, ul-h

Fig. 183. Solitude, c.1923, 7¾ x 12, no copyright information

Fig. 184. Persian Cat, c.1923, 16⅞ x 13⅝, ur-7, ul-h

Fig. 185. Lassitude, *Lassitude*, c.1923, 9 x 11⅜, no copyright information

Fig. 186. Friends, c.1923, 17⅛ x 20⅜, no
copyright information ★

Fig. 187. Geese, c.1923, 10 x 13⅝, no
copyright information ★

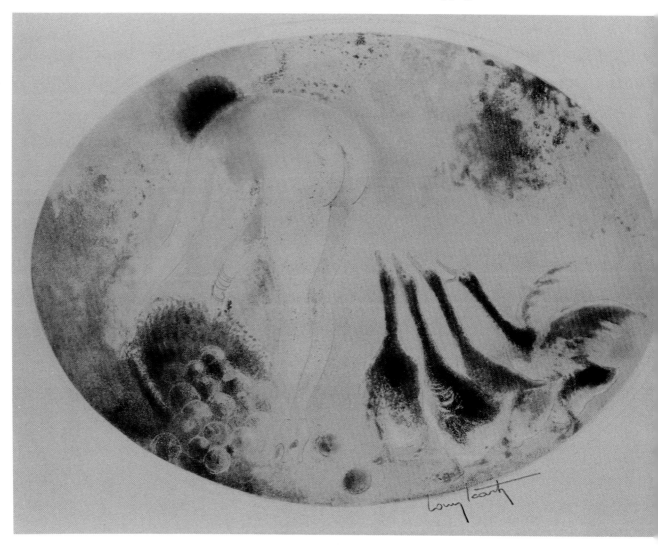

Fig. 188. Pals, 1923, 16¼ x 20½, ul-10, ★

Fig. 189. Success, *La Réussite*, c.1923, 15⅜ x 19⅛, no copyright information ★

94

Fig. 191A. Summer Shade, c.1923, 12¾ x 15¾, no copyright information

Fig. 190. Yellow Blossoms, c.1923, 7⅛ x 10⅛, no copyright information

Fig. 191. Purple Blossoms, c.1923, 7¼ x 10⅛, no copyright information

Fig. 192. Motorcar, *En Auto*, 1923, 14¼ x 18½, ul-10 ★

Fig. 193. Wistfulness, *La Falque*, 1924, 11¾ x 16¾, ul-10a

Fig. 194. Broken Green Jug, *L'Accident*,
c.1923, 17¼ x 12½, ur-7, ul-h ★

Fig. 195. First Snow, c.1922, size unknown

Fig. 197. Welcome Companions, c.1924, 14½ x 9¾, ur-7, ul-j

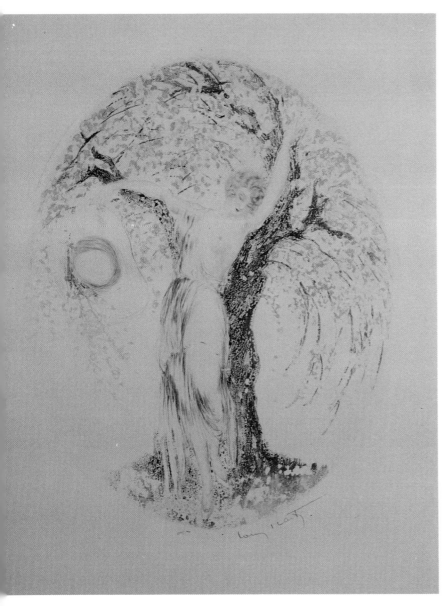

Fig. 196. Springtime, *L'Arbre*, 1924, 18 x 14¼, ur-12 ★

Fig. 198. Baby Doll, *La Poupée*, 1924, 17½ x 13, ul-12

Fig. 199. Chilly One, *Frileuse*, 1924, 17 x 11¼, ul-12

Fig. 201. Winter Bouquet, 1924, 16⅝ x 11¼, ur-8, ul-i ★

Fig. 200. Autumn Swirls, 1924, 16⅝ x 11⅝, ur-8, ul-i

Fig. 202. Ball of Yarn, *La Boule de Laine*, 1924,
16 x 20⅜, ul-12 ★

Fig. 203, Old Yarn, *Le Vielle Laine*, 1924, 16 x
20⅜, ul-12 ★

Fig. 204. Fallen Nest, *Le Nid Renversé*, 1924,
14⅞ x 18¾, ur-5, ul-d

Fig. 205. Little Prisoner, *Petite Prisonniere*,
1924, 14¾ x 18¾, ur-5, ul-d

Fig. 206. Invitation, 1924, 17¼ x 11⅜, ul-12

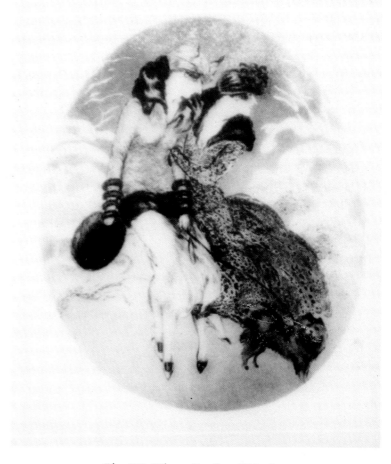

Fig. 208. Winter Stroll, c.1924, size unknown, no copyright information

Fig. 207. Sweet Caress, 1924, 17¼ x 11⅜, ul-12

Fig. 210. Early Harvest, 1924, 18⅞ x 15, ul-12

Fig. 209. Black Cape, c.1924, 13½ x 9, lr-6

Fig. 211. Basket of Apples, *Panier de Pommes*,
1924, 16⅞ x 12¼, ul-12

Fig. 212. Lounging, *Flanerie*, 1924, 13½ x 17¼,
ur-g, ul-12

Fig. 213. Japanese Goldfish, *Poissons Japonais*,
1924, 13⅜ x 17¼, ur-12

Fig. 214. Green Robe, 1924, 13x 17, ul-12

Fig. 215. Laughing Buddha, 1924, 16 x 20½,
ur-8, ul-i

Fig. 216. Blue Garter, 1924, 11⅛ x 8¾, ur-10a

Fig. 217. Black Lace, 1924, 11¼ x 8⅞, ur-12

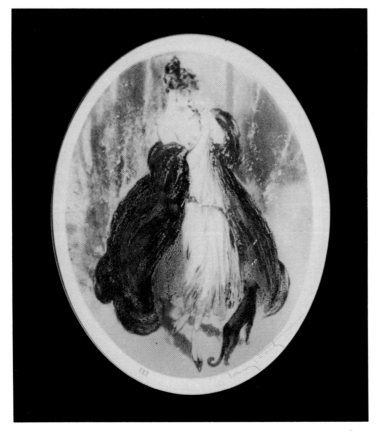

Fig. 218. Garden Stroll, c.1924, 10¾ x 8¼, no copyright information

Fig. 219. New Hat, *Chapeau Nouveau*, 1924, 8¾ x 11¼, ul-10a

Fig. 220. Treasures, *Les Trésors*, 1924, 8⅞ x 11¼, ur-10a

Fig. 221. Diana Coursing, c1924, 16¾ x 21, no copyright information

Fig. 222. Broken Basket, 1924, 16⅞ x 11⅜, ul-12 ★

Fig. 223. Broken Jug, *La Criche Cassée*, 1924,
16⅞ x 11⅜, ul-12

Fig. 224. Make-Up, *Le Maquillage*, 1924, 17⅝ x 13¼, ur-9, ul-k

Fig. 225. Blue Bracelets, *Les Bracelets Bleus*, 1924, 17¾ x 13¼, ur-9, ul-k ★

Fig. 226. Peacock, *Le Paon*, 1925, 18¾ x 14¾,
ul-12

Chapter Four
Late Twenties

1925-1929

Several important changes occurred beginning in 1925 that justify making that date the start of a new period. Elements of method, style and content in works from 1925 are consistent with pieces representing the remainder of the decade.

As Louis Icart's popularity began to explode near the middle of the decade, the edition size produced from each plate was increased to meet the demand. While we estimate that approximately 300 pieces were printed for each etching of 1924, several enormously successful works were created in 1925 that far exceeded that total. "Laziness," "Spilled Milk," and "Puppies" were all printed to the limits of their plates' abilities. Icart abandoned the use of edition notations once and for all.

The great majority of etchings printed between 1924 and 1927 were copyrighted by Les Graveurs Modernes, an art distributor located in Paris. In the last few years of the decade, Icart obtained his own copyrights directly under the names "L.Icart" or "Louis Icart".

The period of the Late Twenties brought into being the etching that we now consider classic Icart. The woman was a tantalizing mix of innocence and seductiveness in her apparent mood. A paradox of soft, simple beauty and bold elegance. The contrasts made one want, wonder, and muse. No longer was the Icart Girl obscured by oppressive bundles of clothing, but rather she preferred being held back only by some translucent wisp of silk. She lounged in the privacy of some secret room heaped to excess with pillows of soft, alluring textures. Those simple bedroom scenes from the Early Twenties now galvanized into the ultimate works of composition and sensual implication. "White Underwear," "Smoke," and "Eve" are good examples of Icart etchings that gave definition to the genre thereafter.

By this point in his career, Icart had mastered a wide variety of techniques in the Aquatint method. This allowed him to set the exact mood and depth required by a wide variety of subjects.

Fig. 227. Red Gate, *La Port Rouge*, 1925, 17⅛ x 12¼, ul-12

Fig. 227A. Icart's Late Signature (c.1926 and Later)

Fig. 228. Awakening, *Le Lever*, 1925, 14⅞ diameter, uc-j

Fig. 229. Retiring, *Le Coucher*, 1925, 14⅞ diameter, uc-j★

Objects and scenery were explored with a greater artistic fervor than in past phases of his career. The simple backdrop of a folding screen would become an intriguing artwork in itself, composed of varied shadows, forms, and textures. The whole spectacle of Paris would unfold in panorama behind Mimi Pinson. From this point on, the Icart Girl had full freedom to revel in a world of color, movement, and energy.

One of the most astonishing aspects of the Late Twenties period is the breadth of imagination that allowed Icart such a diversity of subjects and settings. His works run the gamut from plain to extravagant, historical to modern, tame to risqué. The buyer on the one hand, might have chosen a fully clothed woman sitting sedately amidst a flock of sheep, or may, on the other hand, have purchased a nude giggling about some fantasy on satin sheets. The spectrum available to Icart's consumers is a clear indication of the artist's desire to tap the entire market regardless of individual limits of morality. Clearly, a good portion of the public allowed for Icart's explorations into naughtiness and nudity. Those etchings with just the proper amount of exposure and the proper idea behind them were bought in large numbers. The runaway popularity of "Eve" and "Venus" make that case, both then and now. When the realism became so stark that buyers could make no excuse for the scene, the work sold poorly; such as in the case of "Conchita."

Fig. 230. Icart's "Windmill"(Embossed Seal)

Fig. 231. Anticipation, 1925, 20½ x 26⅜, ul-12

Fig. 233. Ballerina in the Wings, c.1925, 15½ x 9½, no copyright information ★

Fig. 232. Ballerina on Point, c.1925, 15½ x 9½, no copyright information ★

Fig. 234. Madame Tambelli de la Opera, c.1925, 18½ x 12¾, no copyright information

Fig. 235. Gust of Wind, *Coup de Vent*, 1925,
21⅛ x 17⅝, ul-12

Fig. 236. Black Shawl, *Le Chaple Noir*, 1925
16¼ x 11½, ul-12

Fig. 237. Wishing Well, 1925, 16⅞ x 11¼,
ul-12

Fig. 238. New Friends, 1925, 14 x 17¼, ul-12
★

Fig. 239. Shepherd Dog, *Le Berger*, 1925, 17½
x 14⅛, ul-12 ★

Fig. 240. Parrots, *Perroquets*, 1925, 13⅞ x 18½,
UL-12

Fig. 241. Preferred One, *L'Oiseau Preferere*,
1925, 14 x 18⅜, ur-12

Icart was extremely productive in 1927, creating a series of etchings devoted to operas, fairy tales, and literary figures. This allowed him to tap numerous and diverse subjects of great popularity with the public as a whole. The cultural implications behind the fable depicted might well distract the more staid viewers from some nudity or revelry wrapped into the scene. This series of etchings seemed to have something for everyone. If you liked any kind of woman at all, you'd have to find her here.

Based upon both artistic evolution and productivity, we must consider the Late Twenties to have been Icart's Golden Age. Consumers accepted and purchased his works with dedicated pleasure and desire. It was a phase in which the

Fig. 242. Snowstorm, 1925, 18⅞ x 15⅛, uc-12

Fig. 243. December, *Décembre*, 1925, 18½ x 13⅞, ul-12

artist could finally venture beyond the narrow restrictions of past decades and explore the beauty of women unabashed. He experimented with more innovative textures, designs, lines, and movement. His etchings of "Speed" and "Coursing II" look forward to the works of the Thirties with their bold, swift energy and open space. No longer was something being held back by the older formulas of art. We sense a newfound freedom that encourages an even greater expansion. Icart himself is hereafter coursing with some enraptured vision toward triumph on the horizon. In the upcoming Thirties such imagination would exhault itself in stunning creations.

Fig. 244. Bluebirds, *Les Oiseaus Bleues*, 1925, 18⅞ x 15, ul-12

Fig. 245. Rain, *L'Averse*, 1925, 18½ x 13¾, ul-12 ★

119

Fig. 246. Laziness,
Paresse, 1925, 15 x 19,
ul-12

Fig. 247. White
Underwear, *Sur Le
Divan*, 1925, 14¾ x 19,
ul-12

120

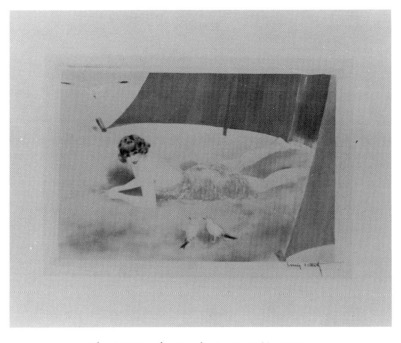

Fig. 248. On the Beach, *Sur Le Sable*, 1925,
10⅜ x 15½, ul-12

Fig. 249. On the Green, *Sur L'Berbe*, 1925,
10½ x 15¾, ul-12 ★

Fig. 250. Before the Raid, *Avant Le Raid*,
1925, 17¼ x 21¼, ul-12 ★

Fig. 251. Bedtime, 1925, 17⅛ x 12¾, lr-9, ll-j
★

Fig. 252. Little Book, *Petit Livre*, 1925, 17¼ x 12¾, lr-9, ll-j

Fig. 253. Spilled Jug of Milk, 1925, 17⅛ x 11½, ul-12

Fig. 254. Puppies, *Petits Chiens*, 1925, 16½ x
20⅞, ur-12

Fig. 255. Spilled Milk, 1925, 16⅜ x 20⅞, ul-12
★

Fig. 256. Fishbowl, 1925, 17⅜ x 11½, ul-12

Fig. 258. Sunset, c. 1926, size unknown, no copyright information

Fig. 257. Elephants, *Les Eléphants*, 1925, 16½ x 11¾, ul-12 ★

Fig. 259 Japanese Garden, *Le Jardin Japonais,*
1925, 14¼ x 17⅜, ul-12

Fig. 260. Fanny & Cat, 1926, 14¼ x 13⅛,
ul-12

Fig. 261. Impudence, *Effronterie*, 1926, 17¾ x 13¼, ul-12 ★

Fig. 262. Teasing, *Taquinerie*, 1926, 17⅞ x 13⅜, ul-12 ★

Fig. 264. Forbidden Fruit, *Fruit Défendu* 1926, 16½ x 12, ul-12

Fig. 263. He Loves Me, He Loves Me Not, *Il M'Aime*, 1926, 16¾ x 12, ur-12

Fig. 265. Coach, 1926, 21¼ x 17⅜, ul-12 or no copyright information

Fig. 268. Storyteller, *La Bonne Historie*, 1926, 14⅛ x 17¼,

Fig. 269. Embrace, *L'Etreinte*, 1926, 14¼ x 17¼,

Fig. 266. Temptation, *Tentation*, 1926, 19½ x 14¼, ul-12

Fig. 267. Small Screen, *Petit Jalousie*, 1926, 11⅛ x 16½, ur-12, ⋆

Fig. 270. Spanish Nights, *Nuit Espagnole*,
1926, 20¾ x 13, ul-12

Fig. 271. Venetian Nights, *Nuit Venitienne*,
1926, 20¾ x 13, ul-12

Fig. 272. Nijinsky, c.1926, size unknown, no
copyright information

Fig. 273. Birds of July, *Les Juillards*, 1926,
18½ x 10¾, ur-12, ★

Fig. 274. Swallows, *Les Hirondelles*, 1926, 18⅝ x
10¾, ul-12

Opposite page:
Fig. 277. Singing
Lesson, *Lêcon de
Chant*, 1926, 13¾ x
18¼, ul-12

Fig. 278.
Pekinese Buddha,
1926, 13¼ x 18⅞,
ur-12★

Fig. 275. Smoke, *Fumée*, 1926, 14⅛ x 19⅜,
ur-12

Fig. 276. Silk
Robe, *La Robe de Chine*,
1926, 15 x 18¼, ul-12★

Fig. 279. Seagulls, *Les Mouettes*, 1926, 20 x 15⅞, ur-12

Fig. 281. Summer Birds, c.1926, size unknown

Fig. 280. Thieves, *Les Pillards*, 1926, 16½ x 12, ul-12 ★

Fig. 282. Open Cage, *La Cage Ouvert*, 1926, 12⅜ x 16⅞, ur-12

Fig. 283. Masks, *Les Masques*, 1926, 18⅝ x 14⅜, ul-12

Fig. 284. Tea, *Le Thé*, 1926, 18⅝ x 14⅜, ur-12

135

Fig. 285. Blossom Time, 1926, 14 x 18½,
ul-12

Fig. 286. Little Butterflies, *Petits Papillons*,
1926, 14¼ x 18¾, ur-12 ★

Fig. 287. Desire, *Ponvoites*, 1926, 13⅛ x 19,
ul-12

Fig. 288. White Wings, 1926, 16¾ x 11¾, ur-
12 ★

Fig. 289. Love Letters,
Lettres D'Amour, 1926, 14 x
18½, ur-12

Fig. 290. Solitaire, 1926, 14
x 18¼, ul-12★

Opposite page:
Fig. 291. French Doll,
Poupé Moderne, 1926, 14 x 18

Fig. 292. Confidence, *La
Confidance,* 1926, 16 x 20⅜,
ul-12

Fig. 293. Alms, *L'Aumône*, 1926, 16¾ x 12⅝,

Fig. 294. Autumn Leaves, *Feuilles D'Automne*, 1926, 20 x 15¾, ul-12

Fig. 295. Forsythia, 1925, 18¾ x 14½, ul-12

Fig. 296. Gossip, *Bavardage*, 1926, 16¾ x 13,

Fig. 297. Bathers, *Baigneuses*, 1926, 20½ x 17¼, ur-5, ul-d ★

Fig. 298. Backstage, c.1926, 11 x 7⅞, no copyright information

Fig. 299. Little Kittens, *Les Chatons*, 1926,
10⅛ x 9½, ul-12 ★

Fig. 300. Tender Lesson, *Tendre Lêcon*, 1926,
10⅛ x 9½, ur-12

Fig. 301. Jealousy, *La Jalousie*, 1927, 9⅝ x
10⅛, ul-12 ★

Fig. 302. Lesson of Love, *Lècon D'Amour*,
1927, 9⅝ x 10⅛, ul-12

143

Fig. 305. Farewell, *Au Revoir*, 1927, 14⅛ x 18⅞, ur-12

Fig. 306. Waiting, *L'Attende*, 1927, 14 x 18⅞, ur-12 ★

Fig. 303. Crossing, *Le Gúe*, 1926, 18⅝ x 13½, ur-12

Fig. 304. Fruit, *Les Fruits*, 1926, 14 x 19¾, ur-12 ★

Fig. 307. My Secret love, 1927, 18¼ x 14½, ul-12

Fig. 308. Hiding Place, *La Cachette*, 1927, 18⅜ x 14½, ur-12

Fig. 310. Snack, *Le Goûter*, 1927, 17¾ x 13¼,
ur-n, ul-15 ★

Fig. 309. Mealtime, *Petit Déjeuner*, 1927, 17¾ x
13¼,ur-n, ul-15

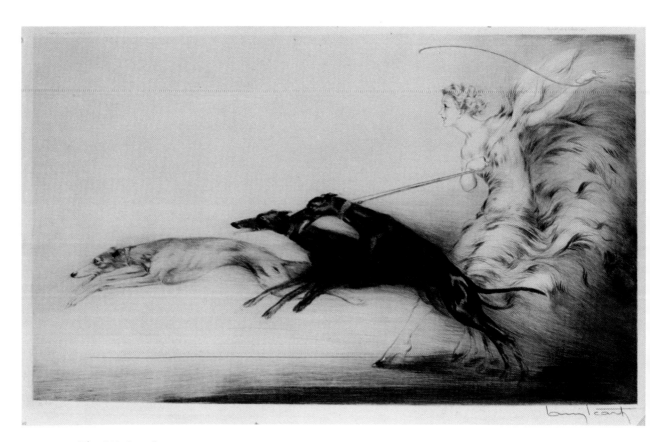

Fig. 311. Speed, *Vitesse*, 1927, 14¾ x 24⅞, ur-15, ul-l

Fig. 312. Thaïs, *Thaïs*, 1927, 16 x 20⅜, ur-12

Fig. 313. Red Riding Hood, *Le Chaperon Rouge*, 1927, 20⅛ x 13¼, ur-15, ul-n

Fig. 314. Little Bo Peep, *Il Pleut Bergère*, 1927, 20¼ x 13½, ur-15, ul-f ★

Fig. 315. Carmen, *Carmen*, 1927, 20⅛ x 13½, ul-12

Fig. 317. Louise, *Louise*, 1927, 20 x 13⅛, ul-12

Fig. 316. Madame Butterfly, 1927, 20 x 13¼, ur-12

Fig. 319. Musetta, *Musetta*, 1927, 20 x 13¼, ur-12

Fig. 318. Mimi, *Mimi*, 1927, 20⅛ x 13¼, ul-12

Fig. 320. Pierrette, *Au Clair de la Lune*, 1927,
20¼ x 13⅛, ur-15, ul-f ★

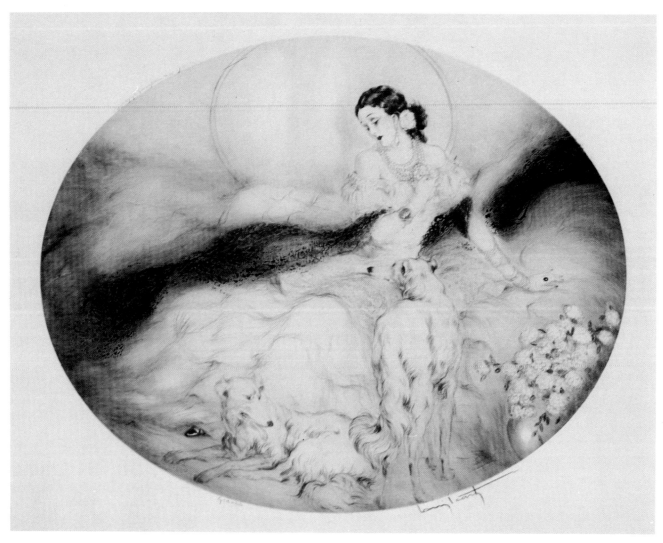

Fig. 321. Lady of the Camelias, *La Dame aux Camélias*, 1927, 16¼ x 20¼, ul-12

Fig. 322. Scheherezade, *Scheherazade*, 1927, 13⅜ x 20⅜, ul-12

Fig. 323. Sleeping Beauty, *La Belle Au Bois Dormant*, 1927, 14¾ x 18½, ur-15, ul-m

Fig. 324. Cinderella, *Cendrillon*, 1927, 14⅝ x 18¼, ur-15, ul-m

Fig. 325. Miss America, 1927, 20⅜ x 16, ul-12

Fig. 326. Miss California, 1927, 20¼ x 15⅞,
ur-12

Fig. 326A. Mischievious, *Les Espìègles*, 1927,
16¼ x 20½, ur-12 ★

Fig. 327. Mimi Pinson, *Mimi Pinson*, 1927 13¼ x 20⅜, ur-12

Fig. 328. Manon, *Manon*, 1927, 20⅛ x 13¼, ur-12

Fig. 329. Mignon, *Mignon*, 1928, 20⅜ x 13⅜, ul-12

Fig. 330. Don Juan, *Don Juan*, 1928, 20¼ x 13¼, ur-15, ul-p

Fig. 331. Casanova, *Casanova*, 1928, 20¼ x 13⅜, ur-15, ul-p

Fig. 332. Swing, *L'Escarpolette*, 1928, 18¾ x
13⅛, ur-n, ul-15

Fig. 333. Meditation, *Dans Les Rêves*, 1928,
11¾ x 16½,ur-15, ul-p

Fig. 334. Recollections,
Dans Les Passés, 1928, 12
x 16½, ur-15, ul-p

Fig. 335. Chestnut Vendor, *Marchande de Marrons*, 1928, 18⅞ x 14, ur-l, ul-15

Fig. 336. Flower Seller, *Marchande de Fleurs*, 18½ x 14¼, ur-l, ul-15

Fig. 337. Look, *Regarde*, 1928, 18⅜ x 14, ur-15, ul-f ★

Fig. 338. Listen, *Ecouté*, 1928, 18⅜ x 13⅞, ur-15, ul-f

Fig. 340. Blue Parrot, *Perroquet Bleu*, 1928, 11¼ x 8⅞, ur-q, ul-15 ★

Fig. 339. Red Cage, *La Cage Rouge*, 1928, 11¼ x 8⅞, ur-q, ul-15 ★

Fig. 341. Spring, *Printemps*, 1928, 8⅞ x 6⅝, ur-l, ul-15

Fig. 342. Summer, *L'Eté*, 1928, 8⅞ x 6⅝, ur-l, ul-15

Fig. 343. Autumn, *Automne*, 1928, 9 x 6¾, ur-15, ul-l

Fig. 344. Winter, *L'Hiver*, 1928, 9 x 6¾, ur-l, ul-15

Fig. 345. Tennis, *Tennis*, 1928, 18⅝ x 13⅝, ul-15

Fig. 346. Zest, *L'Elan*, 1928, 19¼ x 14¼, ul-15

Fig. 347. Intimacy, *Intimité*, 1928, 14⅞ x 17⅞,
ur-o, ul-15 ★

Fig. 348. Mockery,
Moquerie, 1928, 15¼ x 18¼,
ur-15, ul-p★

Fig. 349. Milkmaid, *La Laitière*, 1928, 19⅜ x 12¾, ur-q, ul-15

Fig. 351. Montmartre, *Montmartre*, 1928, 20⅛ x 13⅜, ur-l, ul-15 ★

Fig. 350. Seville, *Séville*, 1928, 19⅞ x 13¼, ur-15

Fig. 352. Faust, *Faust*, 1928, 20½ x 13, ur-l,
ul-15

Fig. 353. Eve, *Eve*, 1928, 13¼ x 18⅞, ur-q,
ul-15

Fig. 354. Tosca, *Tosca*, 1928, 20½ x 13, ur-l,
ul-15

Fig. 355. Venus, *Venus*, 1928, 13⅜ x 18⅞, ur-
q, ul-15

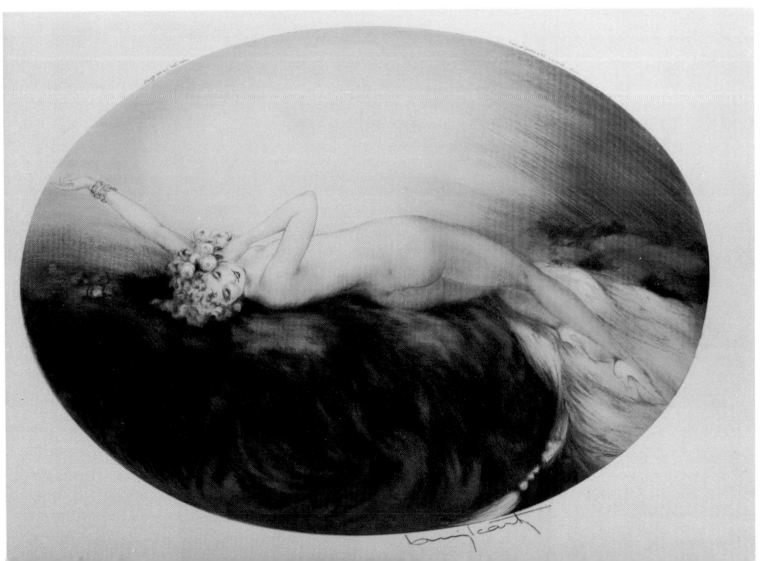

Opposite page:
Fig. 359. Joy of Life, *Joie de Vivre*, 1929, 23⅜ x 15⅛, ul-15

Fig. 356. Poem, *Le Poèm*, 1928, 18⅛ x 21¾, ur-13, ul-15

Fig. 357. Werther, *Werther*, 1928, 20¼ x 13⅜, ur-l, ul-15

Fig. 358. Spilled Apples, *La Panier Renversé*, 1928, 19⅝ x 12½, ur-q, ul-15 ★

Fig. 360. Parasol, 1928, 17½ x 14¼, ur-15, ul-q *

Fig. 362. Ballet, *Ballet*, 1929, 20¼ x 13¼,

Fig. 361. Conchita, *Conchita*, 1929, 20¼ x 13¼, ul-15

Fig. 364. Apache Dancer, *Danse Apache*, 1929,
20¼ x 13¼, ur-15b, ul-r ⋆

Fig. 363. Minuet, *Menuet*, 1929, 20¼ x 13⅜,
ur-15a, ul-r

Fig. 365. Spanish Dance, *Danse Espagnole*,
1929, 20¼ x 13½, ur-15b, ul-r

Fig. 366. Eighteen-Thirty,
1830, 1929, 14⅝ x 17⅝, ur-15

Fig. 367. Nineteen-Thirty,
1930, 1929, 14⅝ x 17½, ur-15★

Fig. 368. Picnic, *Abat-Jour*, 1929, 33¾ x 9, no
copyright information

Fig. 369. Four Dears, *La Biche Apprivoisée*,
1929, 21¼ x 15, ur-f, ul-15 ★

Fig. 370. Dollar, *Mon Chien*, 1929, 9⅝ x 10, ur- 15 ★

Opposite page:
Fig. 372. Sapho, *Sapho,* 1929, 15⅞ x
20¼, ur-15

Fig. 373. Hydrangeas, *Les Hortensias,*
1929, 16¼ x 20¼, ul-15 ★

Fig. 371. Coursing II, *Coursing II,*
1929, 15¼ x 25¼, ul-15

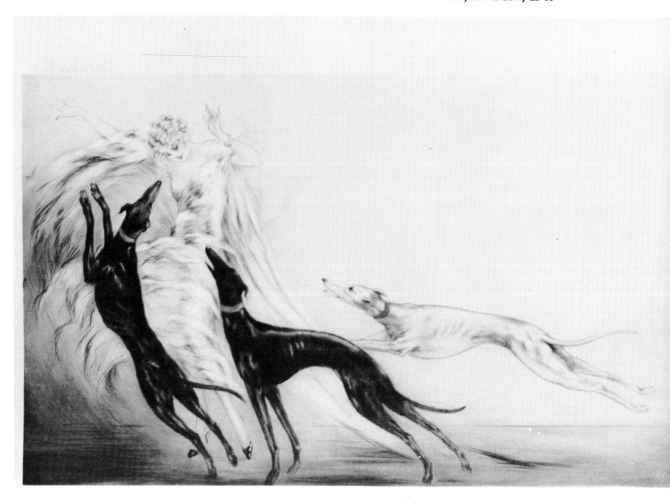

Opposite page:
Fig. 374. After the Walk, *Retour de Promenade*, 1929, 14½ x 18¼, ul-15

Fig. 375. Leaving Home, 1929, 14¾ x 18½, ur-15

Right:
Fig. 376. Pink Alcove, *L'Alcôve Bleue*, 1929, 10¼ x 12⅝, ul-15★

Below:
Fig. 377. Blue Alcove, *L'Alcôve Bleue*, 1929, 10¼ x 12¾, ul-15★

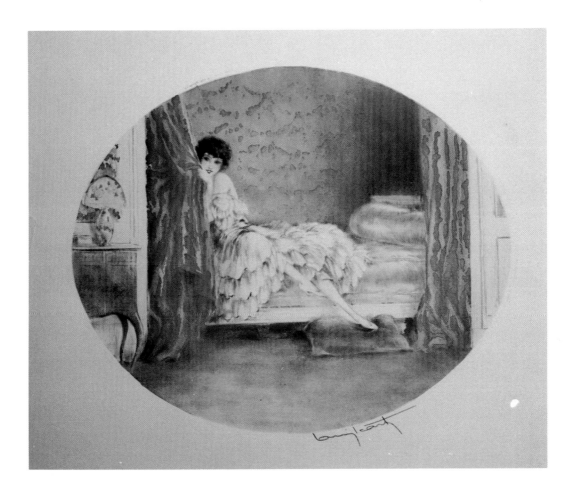

Fig. 378. Bird Seller, *Marchande de Oiseaux*, 18½ x 14⅛, UL-15

Fig. 380. Angry Buddha, *Colère*, 1929, 20½ x 16, ur-9, ul-h

Fig. 379. Orange Seller, *Marchande de Oranges*, 1929, 18½ x 14, ur-15

Fig. 381. Chilly Ones, *Les Frileux*, 1929, 17⅛ x 12¾, ur-15

Fig. 382. Duet, *Le Duo*, 1929, 17⅛ x 13¼, ur-15 ★

Fig. 383. On the Quais, *Sur Les Quais*, 1929,
12¾ x 6, ul-15 ★

Fig. 385. Young Mother, *La Jeune Mère*,
1929, 11¼ x 15⅜, ur-15a ★

Fig. 384. Place Vendome, *Place Vendòe*, 1929,
12¾ x 6, ur-15

Fig. 386. Wounded Dove, *La Colombe Blessée*, 1929, 20½ x 16⅛, ul-15

Fig. 387. Joan of Arc, *Jeanne d'Arc*, 1929, 19 x 14⅝, ur-15

Fig. 388. Salomé, *Salome*, 1928, 20½ x 13⅜, ur-15

Fig. 389. Dalila, *Dalila*, 1929, 20⅜ x 13½, ur-15

Fig. 390. Madame Bovary, *Madame Bovary*, 1929, 16 x 20½, ur-15

Fig. 391. Dear Friends, *Chien et Chat*, 1929, 11⅛ x 8⅞, ul-15 ★

Fig. 392. Dreaming, *Rêverie*, 1938, 24¾ x 17,
ul-16

Chapter Five
The Thirties

1930-1939

The works that Louis Icart created in the Thirties have the most popularity with modern collectors. They draw everyone into their web of allure. They are power-packed works in regards to composition, style, and visual effect. Icart had learned well after twenty years of observing the public what pleased their eyes and imagination. Consequently, a majority of the "key" pieces of the field are products of this decade; a virtual "Who's Who" of rarity and top price.

As always, it remains uncertain how many pieces were actually produced from each plate. However, it seems evident from the painfully small numbers available on the modern market that, overall, the totals were less than in the Twenties. We can only speculate on this discrepancy. Perhaps the financial crisis of 1929, with the ensuing Depression, put luxuries such as artwork out of the reach of families suddenly left struggling. Whatever the cause, the supply is far too limited to meet the demands of modern collectors.

The works from this period were largely copyrighted through the New York Graphic Society of New York City. This firm apparently had exclusive rights to distribute most of Louis Icart's etchings in the United States during the Thirties. Small catalogues with photographs of the most popular Icarts were supplied to retail galleries across the country. Prices for unframed works ranged from $6 to $20. Though the higher figures were sizable amounts during the Depression, the strong decorative appeal of Thirties works may have justified the apparent extravagance.

In general, during this decade Icart's etchings increased in size. Regardless of the specific subject, the pieces became more grand and imposing. The emotional and visual effect were both magnified. These pieces fit well into the more open rooms that seemed to be the trend of the Deco period.

Icart's women were finally liberated completely.

Fig. 393. Lovers, *Des Grieux*, 1930, 20½ x 13⅝, ur-15a

Fig. 394. Laughing, *Rieuse*, 1930, 11⅜ x 16⅜, ul-15

Fig. 395. Sulking, *Boudeuse*, 1930, 11¼ x 16⅜, ul-15a

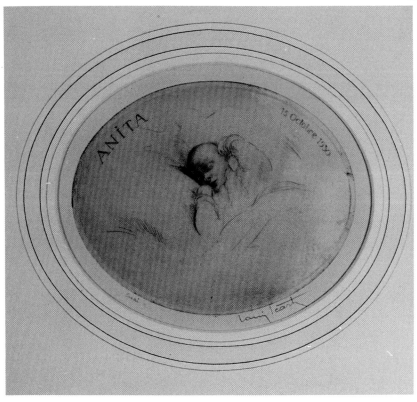

Fig. 396. Anita, 1930, 6 x 7½, no copyright information ★

Fig. 397. Pink Dress, *Robe Rose*, 1930, 5¾ x 8,
ur-15

Fig. 398. Good Pickings, 1930, 6½ x 9, ur-15

Fig. 399. Pet, 1930, 5¼ x3½, ur-15

Fig. 400. Paris Flowers,
Fleurs de Paris, 1930, 18¾ x
15, ul-15a

Fig. 401. Golden Veil,
Méditation, 1930, 15 x 19,
ul-15a★

188

Fig. 402. Coursing III, *Coursing III*, 1930, 15⅜ x 25⅛, ul-15★

Fig. 403. Cigarette Memories, *Cigarette*, 1931, 14⅜ x 17⅝, ur-15★

189

Fig. 404. Bubbles, *Les Bulles*, 1930, 17¼ x 12¼,
ur-15

While still thoroughly beautiful in the eyes of admiring men, they seemed more determined to direct their own destiny. They were more of everything; stronger willed, more elegant, and more difficult to predict. When presented as nudes they are proud and unashamed. They seem little bothered by what judgements the observer might be passing. They are strong enough to stand on their own as the central focus of any picture; such as in "Waltz Echoes," "Dreaming," and "Wisteria." And in fact, in "Ecstasy," the impassioned blonde has fully transcended any concerns with the outside world. She is no longer a passive object or spectacle. The desire and imagination are now all hers. Finally the Icart Girl has become a woman who won't be held down on paper!

Fig. 405. Rainbow, *Arc en Ciel*, 1930, 24¾ x 17, ul-15

Fig 406. Black Fan, *Eventail Noir*, 1931, 16⅛ x 20¾, ur-15

Fig. 409. Youth, *Jeunesse*, 1930, 23⅞ x 15⅜, ul-15a

Fig 409A Hello, *Au Telephone*, c.1930, 6⅝ x 4¼, no copyright information

Fig. 407. Bathing Beauties, *Baigneuses*, 1931, 24¾ x 16⅞, ul-15 ★

Fig. 408. D'Artagnan, *D'Artagnan*, 1931, 20⅜ x 13½, ur-15

Fig. 410. Venus in the Waves (light blue),
La Vague, 1931, 19 x 15⅜, ur-15 ★

Within this progressive decade, Icart is still capable of producing works that largely depend on the formulas of the Twenties. In "Charm of Montmartre," he carries the use of detail and color to the maximum degree possible for such a formula of composition. And yet the Thirties stand out as special because Icart took many of his early ideas down experimental paths. He created new and stunning effects with pictures set in vast, open expanses of nature. As the decade proceeded, Icart's representation of countryside became more vibrant in its colors, panoramic in its open depth, and impressionistic in both texture and detail. The world in which Icart's women lounged was a large, stunning spectacle. "Summer Dreams" and "Swans" illustrate the romanticism Icart's could now conjure.

Throughout earlier phases of his career, objects in his etchings were stationary for the most part. The Thirties brings motion to Icart's works. "Venus in the Waves," "Yachting," and "Mardi Gras" are stunning examples of this energetic style. "Thoroughbreds" might be considered the epitome.

Fig. 411. Venus in the Waves (dark blue),
La Vague, 1931, 19 x 15⅜, ur-15 ★

193

Fig. 412. Finale, *Finale*, 1931, 18¾ x 15, ur-15
★

Fig. 413. Memory, *Le Souvenir*, 1931, 16⅜ x 19½, no copyright information ★

Fig. 414. Bird in the Tempest, *L'Oiseau dans la Tempête*, 1931, 26¾ x 20⅛, *no copyright information* ★

Fig. 416. Flight To Freedom, c.1931, 18 x 13, no copyright information

Fig. 415. White Bird, *L' Oiseau Blanc*, c. 1931, 26⅝ x 15, no copyright information

Opposite page:
Fig. 419. Two Beauties, *Lex Yeux*, 1931, 16¾ x 24⅝, ul-15

Fig. 420. Belle Rose, *Les Roses*, 1933, 16¼ x 20⅞, ul-16

Fig. 417. Perfect Harmony, *Accord Parfait*, 1932, 12½ x 16½, ur-16b

Fig. 418 Martini, *Cocktail*, 1932, 12½ x 16½, ur-16 ★

Fig. 421. Charm of Montmartre, *Vieux Montmartre*, 1932, 20½ x 13⅞, ul-16a ★

Fig. 422. Spring Blossoms, *Fleurs de Nire*, 1932, 23¼ x 15⅛, ur-16a ★

Fig. 423. My Model, *Modèle*, 1932, 21⅛ x 16½, ur-16 ★

Fig. 424. Modern Eve, *Modèle II*, 1933, 21⅛ x 16½, ur-16 ★

Fig. 425. Speed II, *Vitesse*, 1933, 15 x 24¾, ul-16

Fig. 426. Symphony in White, *Blancheurs*,
1932, 18⅞ x 15, ul-16 ★

Fig. 428. Unmasked, *Paravent Rouge*, 1933,
12¼ x 8⅛, ur-16

Fig. 427. Masked, *Masque Noir*, 1933, 12⅜ x
8⅛, ur-16 ★

Fig. 429. Love's Awakening, *Le Pomme*, 1933, 8 x 10⅞, ul-16a ★

Fig. 430. Pink Lady, *La Dame Rose*, 1933, 8¼ x 10⅞, ul-16 ★

Fig. 431. Summer Dreams, *Vacances*, 1934, 19⅝ x 17⅝, ul-16 ★

Icart began to make greater use of sharp contrasts in color and tone between his model and her background. A backdrop of sepia is used in "Melody Hour." A complex, dark pattern is employed in "Orchids" and "Lilies" to achieve a similar effect. This visual device reaches its ultimate application in etchings using a solid black backdrop as the entire space behind the figure. In "Love's Blossom," "Bubbles," and "Illusion", this technique serves to spotlight the models. Subtle colors and textures appear enhanced by their proximity to such total darkness. This contrast challenges and stirs the eye.

Fig. 432. Music Room (document), c.1934,
15⅛ x 18⅞, ul-15c

Fig. 433. Grande Eve, *Grande Eve*, 1934, 30½
x 19¾, ul-16 ★

Fig. 434. Music Room, 1934, 12⅜ x 15¼, ul-
15c ★

Fig. 435. Swimmer (printed on wood),
Nageuse, c.1934, 18⅝ x35, no copyright
information

Fig. 436. Leda & the Swan, *Léda*, 1934, 19⅞
x30½, ul-16

Fig. 437. Melody Hour, *Quatour*, 1934, 18⅛ x
22⅞, ul-16

Fig. 438. Repose, *Sommeil*, 1934, 18⅝ x 45½,
ur-16a

Fig. 439. Ballerina, *Repos*, 1935, 14⅛ x 18,
ul-16

Fig. 440. Hoopla, *Hop-La*, 1935, 8 x 10⅞, ul-16

Fig. 441. Peonies, *Pivoines*, 1935, 8¼ x 11, ul-16

Fig. 442. N.Y. Graphic Society (Embossed Seal)

Fig. 443. Ecstasy, *Volupté*, 1935, 16⅝ x 15, ur-16

Fig. 444. Winsome, *Candeur*, 1935, 16¾ x 15, ul-16

Fig. 445. Can Can, *Can-Can Française*, 1935,
15¾ x 24¾, ul-16 ★

Fig. 446. Follies, *Folies*, 1935, 15¾ x 24⅞, ur-16

210

Fig. 447. Sweet Mystery,
Enigme, 20⅝ x 16, cl-16

Fig. 448. Soda Fountain, *Au
Restaurant*, 1935, 21⅜ x 15⅝,
ul-16★

What is most satisfying about the Thirties works is their variety of inspiration and imagination. They have evolved from some wholly new person. The series of dog caricatures arrived, pitting elegant women against shaggy misfits in "Martini," "Gay Trio," and "Perfect Harmony". The bold and liberated nudes, such as "Modern Eve," stepped into the spotlight with unshakable pride and certainty. The outdoors burst forth in a dazzling bloom of color and energy, as if fed by some new kind of rain. Women became more elegant than we could imagine in "Sofa" and "Love's Blossom". They became thoughtful and sensitive to a depth that surprised us in "Waltz Dreams." Full of talent and bravado, some wooed our hearts in "Melody Hour" and "Waltz Echo".

Fig. 449. Yachting, *Yachting*, 1936, 18¾ x 24¾,
ul-16

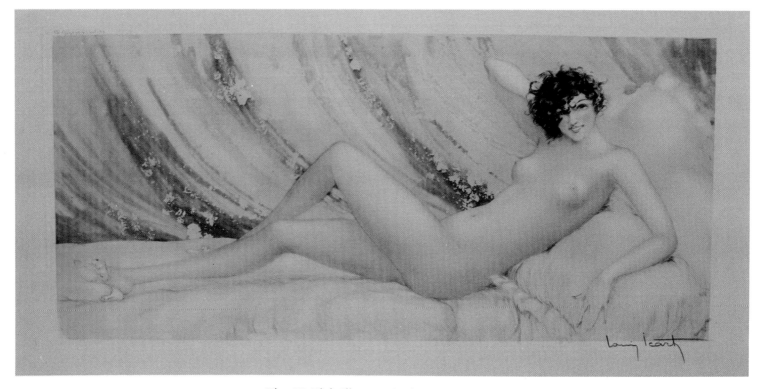

Fig. 450. Pink Slippers, *Rèveil*, 1936, 11 x 24½,
ul-14

Fig. 451. Favorite, *Brebis et Agneau,*
1936, 14¾ diameter, ur-16

Fig. 452. Guardians, *Berger et
Bèrgere,* 1936, 14¾ diameter, ur-16

Fig. 453. Fluttering Butterfly, *Papillon I*,
1936,6½ x 8¾, ul-16

And behind their deep, sensuous eyes, we sense the full splendor of the soul in "Two Beauties." Still, they could please, allure and amuse. Taken as a whole, the etchings of the Thirties are almost too much to digest or comprehend. Their technical ability and visual impact draw forth our every emotion. We cannot ignore a single part of ourselves, no matter how deep or well hidden, for Icart pulls all feelings forth. It is so easy to surrender our hearts and minds to his ladies who themselves hold nothing back.

Fig. 454. Open Wings, *Papillon II*, 1936, 6½ x 8¾, ul-16

Fig. 455. Woman in Wings, *Papillon III*, 1936,
6⅜ x 8¾, ul-16

Fig. 456. Corseted Butterfly, *Papillon IV*,
c.1936, 6¾ x 8¾, no copyright information

Fig. 457. Gay Trio, *Au Bar*, 1936, 18⅜ x 10⅞, ul-16

Fig. 458. Mardi Gras, *A La Fête*, 1936, 18⅝ x 18¼, ul-16

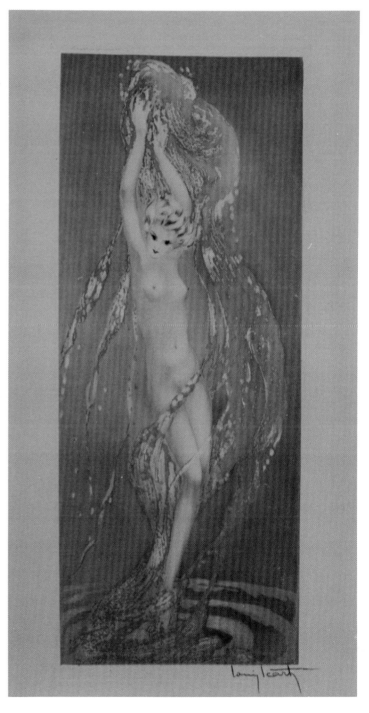

Fig. 459. Waterfall, *La Source*, 1936, 20⅛ x 8¼, ul-16

Fig. 460. Fountain, *Le Jet D'Eau*, 1936, 20⅛ x 8¼, ul-16

Fig. 461. Symphony in Blue, *Symphonie en Bleu*, 1936, 22⅝ x 18⅞, ul-16

Fig. 462. On the Champs Elysees, *Aux Champs Elysées*, 1938, 15¼ x 21¾, ul-16

Fig. 463. Girl in Crinoline, *Miroir de Venise*,
1937, 22¼ x 18⅞, ul-16

Fig. 464. Fair Dancer, 1939, 18¾ x 22⅛, ur-14

Fig. 465. Love's Blossom, *Parfum de Fleurs*,
1937, 16½ x 24⅝, ur-16

Fig. 466. Orchids, *L'Orchides*, 1937, 27 x 18¾,
ul-16a

Fig. 467. Sofa, *Le Sofa*, 1937, 17 x 25¾, ul-16 ★

Fig. 468. Lilies, *Les Lis*, 1934, 27¾ x 18⅞, ul-14

Fig. 469. Pool, *Reflets*, 1937, 19 x 8¾, ur-16

Fig. 470. Song of the Sea, *Le Coquillage*, 1936,
18¾ x 14⅞, ul-16 ★

Fig. 471. Happy Birthday, 1937, 13⅝ x 18½,
ur-16

Fig. 472. Thoroughbreds, *Pur-Sang*, 1938,
17¾ x34¼, ul-16

Fig. 473. Swans, *Les Cygnes*, 1937, 21⅞ x 18½,
ul-16

Fig. 474. Waltz Dream, *Rêve de Valse*, 1938,
14¼ x 16⅝, ul-14

Fig. 475. Waltz Echoes, *Résonance*, 1938, 19 x
19, ul-16

Fig. 476. Spring Flowers, *Fleurs de Nice*, 1939, 18¾ x 14⅛, ul-14

Fig. 477. Gay Senorita, *Gitane*, 1939, 17½ x 21½, ul-16

Fig. 478. Fair Model, *Première Rose*, 1937, 18¾ x 11⅛, ul-16 ★

Fig. 479. Pink Slip, *L'Essayage*, 1939, 18⅞ x 11⅛, ur-16

Fig. 480. Illusion, *Tabac Blond*, 1940, 18⅞ x 8⅜, ul-14

Chapter Six
The Final Years

1940-1953

Louis Icart's etchings, which began the decade of the Forties appear to be on a direct continuum with works from the late Thirties in regard to style. As a group, the works copyrighted in 1940 are splendid creations relative to their composition, technique, and visual impact. The artist continued to exploit such methods as strong color contrasts, striking imagery and spatial expansiveness. It is a pleasure to recognize Icart's continuing diversity in that he could alternate the creation of a more traditional composition such as "Morning Cup," with the stunning fantasy evoked in "Illusion."

It was inevitable that World War II and Icart's career were on a collision course. Copper became a scarce commodity, limiting the size and number of etchings that could be produced. When France surrendered to Germany in 1940, artwork could no longer be exported to the remaining free world. As a result, Icart was forced to redirect the bulk of his creative energy into his oil paintings. Etchings were limited to smaller pictures made for collectors' books and menu covers. Eventually the Impressionistic style of his oils influenced the composition of his etchings. This became more apparent after the war as in "The Madeleine" and "Summer Music."

The majority of Icart's post-war etchings were constructed for maximum decorative appeal. While most remained Impressionistic, several works recall earlier phases in the artist's career. "Frou Frou" features a central model drawn predominantly in drypoint, much like those from the fashion period. However, she is now set free in a larger space.

Perhaps the most astonishing creation left to us as evidence of Icart's continued genius into the late Forties, is "Horsewoman" or "Amazonia". This work integrates the majority of successful techniques employed by Icart throughout his career. And yet it is the emotional intensity of the rider and her steed that gives this work its power. The woman is spontaneous and yet determined in

Fig. 481. Victory, c.1945, 10 x 7¾, no copyright information

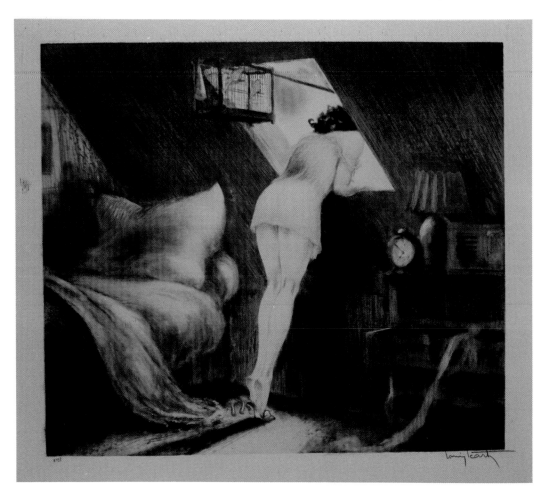

Fig. 482. Attic Room, *Sous le Toit*, 1940, 14⅜ x
16½, ul-17

Fig. 483. Morning Cup, *L'Invitée*, 1940, 19½ x
17½, ul-14

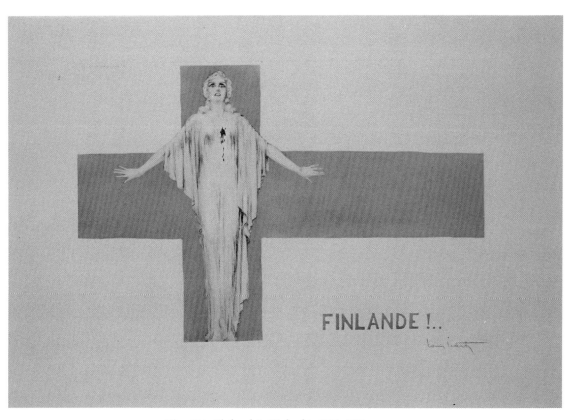

Fig. 484. Finlande!, *Finlande!*, 1940, 14⅛ x
21¼, ul-14

Fig. 485. Arrival, *Arrivée*, 1941, 16⅞ x 11¾,
ul-14

Fig. 486. Departure, *Départ*, 1941, 16⅞ x 11¾,
ur-14

Fig. 487. Southern Charm, *Falbalas*, 1940, 20¼ x 14½, ul-14

Fig. 488. Parasol Twins, 1941, 16½ x 10⅞, ul-14

Fig. 489. Wisteria, *La Glycine*, 1940, 17⅜ x 21¼, ur-14

Fig. 490. Red Fan, 1940, 7⅞ x 10¼, ur-14

Fig. 491. Guest, *L'Invitée*, 1941, 16¾ x 11, ul-14 *

her race to be carefree. The opportunity to find freedom in the open spaces ahead is the immediate challenge. The intensity of her commitment draws forth admiration from the viewer. "Amazonia" reaches a pinnacle that should make any lover of Icart want to sit gazing upon it while in front of a fire, sipping a toasty drink, thinking, purring and feeling content to the core.

There should be no sadness in knowing that "Amazonia" was one of Icart's last etchings before his death. There are few men who have so closely approached such a magical height of success in their lives. "Amazonia" stands as a final tribute for a man most in love with the art of beautiful women. She is his epitaph, so she proceeds as Icart would have wished. In her sturdy beauty she mounts a determined steed; a pet, a friend, a beauty in his own right. She will race, with wind tossing back her hair, blowing her clothes aside a bit, pinking her cheeks from the chill. The speed and fury might brush everything else aside. Soon there is only the beauty of the stallion and his rider. All is distilled down to the purest essence that Icart had taught us: life and its beauty summed up in a woman.

Fig. 492. Frou Frou, *Frou Frou*, 1948, 18⅝ x 15, ur-15

Fig. 493. Motherhood, c. 1934, 17¼ x 20, no copyright information

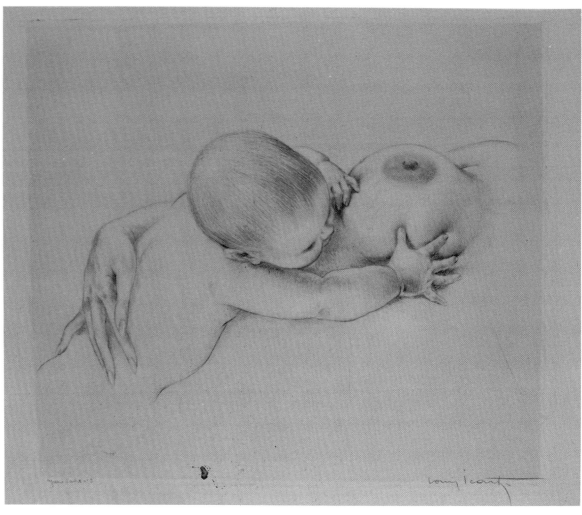

Fig. 494. Lampshade, *La Lampe*, 1948, 14⅞ x
19⅛, ul-15 ★

Fig. 495. Summer Music, 1953,
13¾ x 16¾, ur-20, ul-19a

Fig. 496. Madeleine-Bastille Bus, 1948, 12½ x
16⅞, ur-14

Fig. 497. Clichy-Odeon Bus, 1948, 12½ x
16⅞, ur-14b

Fig. 498. View of Paris, *Paris*, 1949, 5¾ x 8¾,
ur-18

Fig. 499. Paris, *Paris (Vue de Montmartre)*, 1949, 17½ x 26⅞, ur-19, ll-s

Fig. 500. Springtime Promenade, *Promenade au Bois*, 1948, size unknown

Fig. 501. Springtime Promenade, *Promenade au Bois*, 1953, 12¾ x 15¾, ul-14

Fig. 502. Horsewoman, *Amazonia*, 1948, 24¾
x 20¼, ur-15 ★

Appendix I

Title Cross-Reference

—The proper title is in *Italics*
—An asterisk (*) in this reference indicates that though the proper title was not originally given to a work by Icart, it has become so widely used that it is now preferred over the original.

Accident = *Geese*
After the Attack = *After the Raid*
After the Raid = After the Attack
Amazonia = *Horsewoman*
Anita = Baby Anita
At Rest = *Coursing III*
Aunt = *Summer In Yellow*
Baby Anita = *Anita*
Ball of Yarn = Siamese Kitten
Ballerina in the Wings = In the Wings
Ballerina on Point = On Point
Ballerina Repos = *Ballerina*
Ballerina = Ballerina Repos
Bathers = Three Bathers
Bathing Beauties = Four Bathers
Bedtime = Candle
Bedtime = Lighting His Way
Before the Attack = *Before the Raid*
Before the Masquerade = *Venetian Shawl*
Before the Raid = Before the Attack
Bird in the Storm = *Bird in the Tempest*
Bird in the Tempest = Bird in the Storm
Birds of a Feather = *Jealousy*
Birds of July = *Thieves*
Birds of July = Woman With Doves
Birdsong = Duet
Birth of Venus = *Venus in the Waves*
Black Hat = Red Hat
Black Mask = *Masked*
Blue Alcove = Blue Divan
Blue Bandana = *Shepherd Dog*
Blue Bracelets = Bracelets
Blue Buddha (1924) = *Old Yarn*
Blue Buddha (1926) = *Pekinese Buddha*
Blue December = *Winter Bouquet*
Blue Divan = *Blue Alcove*
Blue Parakeets = *On the Branches*
Blue Parrot = Pet
Blue Vanity = *Spanish Comb*
Bountiful Harvest = New Grapes

Bracelets = *Blue Bracelets*
Brittania = Miss Britany
Broken Basket = Spilled Apples (1924)
Broken Blue Jug = Broken Jug (1922)
Broken Green Jug = Broken Jug (c.1923)
Broken Jug (1922) = *Broken Blue Jug*
Broken Jug (c.1923) = *Broken Green Jug*
Butterfly Falls = *Little Butterflies*
Can Can = French Quadrille*
Candle = *Bedtime*
Cat & Mouse = *Incident*
Cat = Playtime
Charm of Montmartre = Montmartre II
Choice Morsel = *Snack*
Cigarette Memories = Cigarette*
Cigarette = *Cigarette Memories**
Coach = *Springtime Promenade*
Cocktail = *Martini*
Conversation = *Seduction*
Coursing III = At Rest
Cuddling = *Small Screen*
Dancer = *Finale*
Dear Friends = Dog & Cat
Dear Friends = Friends
Dog & Cat = *Dear Friends*
Dollar = My Dog
Dream Waltz = *Waltz Dream*
Dressing = *Teasing*
Duet = Birdsong
Eager to Play = *Symphony in White*
Effrontery = *Impudence*
Elephants = Little Elephants
Empty Cage = Open Cage (1922)
Eve & the Serpent = *Grande Eve**
Fair Dancer = Music Hall
Fair Model = First Blush
Fidelity = My Secret Love
Finale = *Dancer*
First Blush = *Fair Model*
First Cherries = *Parasol*

Four Bathers = *Bathing Beauties*
Four Dears = Tamed Hind
French Quadrille = *Can Can**
Friends = *Dear Friends*
Friends = Girl with Peacock
Fruit = Woman with Grapes
Game of Cards = *Success*
Gavotte = Minuet in Rose
Geese = Accident
Girl With Peacock = *Friends*
Golden Veil = Meditation
Grande Eve = Eve & the Serpent*
Green Screen = *Intimacy*
Grenade = *Human Grenade*
Guest = Snacktime
Homage to Guynemere = Over the Wings
Horsewoman = *Amazonia*
Human Grenade = *Grenade*
Hydrangeas = Lilacs
Impudence = Effrontery
In the Open = *On the Green*
In the Wings = *Ballerina in the Wings*
Incident = Cat & Mouse
Intimacy = Green Screen
Japanese Parasol = *Waiting*
Jealousy = Birds of a Feather
Kittens (1926) = *Little Kittens*
Kittens = *Spilled Milk**
Lampshade = Pink Lampshade
Lighting His Way = *Bedtime*
Lilacs = *Hydrangeas*
Lipstick = *Modern Eve*
Little Bo Peep = Shepherdess in the Rain
Little Butterflies = Butterfly Falls
Little Elephants = *Elephants*
Little Eve = *Love's Awakening*
Little Kittens = Kittens (1926)
Look = Secrets
Love's Awakening = Little Eve
Loveseat = *Sofa*

Marianne = Miss France
Martini = Cocktail
Martini = New Spirit
Masked = Black Mask
Meditation = Golden Veil
Memories = Cigarette Memories
Memory = Souvenir
Minuet in Rose = Gavotte
Mischievious = Teasing
Miss Brittany = Britannia
Miss France = Marianne
Mockery = Red Screen
Model I = My Model
Model II = Modern Eve
Modern Eve = Lipstick
Modern Eve = Model II
Montmartre I = Montmartre
Montmartre II = Charm of Montmartre
Mother & Child = Young Mother
Motorcar = Motoring
Motoring = Motocar
Music Hall = Fair Dancer
Music Room = Singing Lesson I
My Dog = Dollar
My Model = Model I
My Secret Love = Fidelity
New Grapes = Bountiful Harvest
New Spirit = Martini
Notre Dame = On the Quais
Old Yarn = Blue Buddha (1924)
On Point = Ballerina on Point
On the Branches = Blue Parake
On the Green = In the Open
On the Quais = Notre Dame
Open Cage (1922) = Empty Cage
Orange Blossom = Soda Fountain
Over the Wings = Homage to Guynemere

Pals = Woman With Borzois
Parasol = First Cherries
Pekinese Buddha = Blue Buddha
Pet = Blue Parrot
Pigeons = White Wings
Pink Alcove = Pink Divan
Pink Divan = Pink Alcove
Pink Lady = Small Hydrangeas
Pink Lampshade = Lampshade
Playtime = Cat
Pool = Reflecting Pool
The Preferred One = Red Cage (1925)
Rain = Shower
Red Cage (1925) = The Preferred One
Red Cage (1928) = Safe At Home
Red Hat = Black Hat
Red Screen = Mockery
Reflecting Pool = Pool
Retiring = Sleepy
Robin = Duet
Safe At Home = Red Cage (1928)
Scared = Surprise
Sea Nymph = Song of the Sea
Secrets = Look
Seduction = Conversation
Serpent & Apple = Grande Eve★
Settee = Sulking
Shepherd Dog = Blue Bandana
Shepherdess in the Rain = Little Bo Peep
Shower = Rain
Siamese Kitten = Ball of Yarn
Singing Lesson II = Music Room
Sleepy = Retiring
Small Hydrangeas = Pink Lady
Small Screen = Cuddling
Snack = Choice Morsel
Snacktime = Guest

Soda Fountain = Orange Blossom
Sofa = Loveseat
Solitaire = Success
Song of the Sea = Sea Nymph
Souvenir = Memory
Spanish Comb = Blue Vanity
Spilled Apples (1924) = Broken Basket
Spilled Apples (1928) = Spilled Peaches
Spilled Milk = Kittens ★
Spilled Peaches = Spilled Apples (1928)
Springtime Promenade = Coach
Success = Solitaire
Success = Game of Cards
Sulking = Settee
Summer Dreams = Vacation ★
Summer In Yellow = Aunt
Surprise = Scared
Symphony in White = Eager to Play
Tamed Hind = Four Dears
Teasing = Dressing
Teasing = Mischievious
Thieves = Birds of July
Three Bathers = Bathers
Vacation = Summer Dreams★
Venetian Shawl = Before the Masquerade
Venus in the Waves = Birth of Venus★
Waiting = Japanese Parasol
Waltz Dream = Dream Waltz
White Lampshade = Lampshade
White Wings = Pigeons
Winter Bouquet = Blue December
Woman With Borzois = Pals
Woman With Doves = Birds of July
Woman With Grapes = Fruit
Young Mother = Mother & Child

Appendix II

Key to Copyright

Most etchings by Louis Icart were copyrighted in the United States and/or France. The copyright information, and sometimes the editor or publisher of the etching was engraved into the copper plate. It can be found either at the very edge of the printed etching, or just above it in the margin. Remember, not all etchings have these notations, especially his early work. It is also possible to find an etching that should have the information, but does not. An artist's proof copy or one printed from an improperly inked plate may be lacking the notation.

At the end of each picture caption is a code used to identify the copyright information for each piece. The first two letters indicate where the information is located on the etching.

Example:
ul—upper left
lr—lower right
cl—center left

Following the locating code is the number or letter from the key which the reader will find in Appendix II, indicating what information is actually printed on the etching.

Example: ul-2. By referring to Appendix II the reader would learn that in the upper left of the etching would be found "Copyright by Wagram, Paris". Where a date appears in the notation, we have substituted *month* or *year*, to keep the total number smaller. There will be some minor variation in the hand engraved notations. If the space is left blank in the picture caption, it is because we believe there is a notation, but not have been able to verify it. "No Copyright Information" appears in the picture captions of those etchings which in our research, never were annotated.

Alternate Titles

An asterisk (*) at the end of a caption indicates that an etching is known by alternate titles. An alphabetical Title Cross Reference is found in Appendix I.

Key to Copyright Notations on Icart Ethings

1. Copyright *year*. Published by Robert Arnot, Paris, London, Vienna, Hamburg. Printed in Paris
2. Copyright by Wagram, Paris
3. Copyright by Jules Hartecoeur et fils, *month*, *year*
3a. Copyright by Jules Hartecoeur & fils Paris, *month*, *year*
3b. Copyright by Jules Hartecoeur Paris *year*
4. Copyright *year* by the F. H. Bresler & Co., Milwaukee, USA
4a. Copyright *year* by the F.H. Bresler Co., Milwaukee, USA
4b. Copyright *year* by the Bresler Co., Milwaukee, USA
5. Copyright *year* by Ste. Ame. l'Estampe Moderne Paris
6. P. Schneider & Cie, Grs, Paris
7. Copyright by Les Graveurs Modernes, Paris
8. Copyright by Les Graveurs Modernes, Paris, *year*
9. Copyright *year* by "Les Graveurs Modernes" Paris
10. Copyright by les Graveurs Modernes, 194 rue de Rivoli, Paris, *year*
10a. Copyright by *year* les Graveurs Moderne. 194 Rue de Rivoli, Paris
11. Copyright by les Graveurs Modernes, 14 Rue de Rivoli, Paris
12. Copyright *year* by les Graveurs Modernes 194 Rue de Rivoli, Paris

13. Copyright by Jaubert & Co. 5 rue Scribe, Paris, *year*

14. Copyright *year* by L. Icart, N.Y.

14a. Copyright *year* L. Icart N.Y.

14b. Copyright *year* by L. Icart, New York

15. Copyright *year* by L. Icart, Paris

15a. Copyright *year* by Louis Icart, Paris

15b. Copyright *year* Louis Icart Paris

15c. Copyright *year* by L. Icart

16. Copyright *year* by L. Icart Sty., N.Y.

16a. Copyright *year* by Louis Icart Sty., N.Y.

16b. Copyright *year* by Louis Icart Soc.ty

17. Copyright *year* by L. Icart, Paris, New York

18. L. Icart Paris *year*

19. Copyright *year* by F. Icart, Paris

19a. Copyright by F. Icart, Paris *year*

20. Copyright Icart, Paris *year*

    a. Ch. Loccard, Editeur 20 rue Drouot, Paris

    b. Edite par Georges Petit. 5 rue DeSeze, Paris, *month, year*

    c. Publie par l'Estampe Moderne, 12 rue Godot de Mauroi, Paris, *year*

    d. Publie par l'Estampe Moderne, 14 rue de Richelieu, Paris *year*

    e. Publie par l'Estampe Moderne, 14 rue de Richelieu, Paris

    f. Edite par l'Estampe Moderne, 14 rue de Richelieu, Paris

    g. Imp. A Porcabeuf & Co., Paris

    h. Edite par la Societie "Les Graveurs Moderne" 194 rue de Rivoli, Paris

    i. Edite par la Societie des Graveurs Moderne 194 rue de Rivoli, Paris

    j. Edite par la Ste les Graveurs Modernes 194 rue de Rivoli, Paris, *year*

    k. Edite par la Ste. Les Graveurs Modernes, 194 rue de Rivoli, Paris

    l. Edite par Les Graveurs Moderne 194 rue de Rivoli, Paris

    m. Edite par les Artistes Modernes 5 rue Scribe, Paris, *year*

    n. Edite par les Artistes Modernes 5 rue Scribe, Paris

    o. Edite par les Editions d Art Devambez 28 Rue Lavoisier, Paris

    p. Editions d'Art Devambez, 23 rue Lavoisier, Paris

    q. Edite par Jaubert et Cie 5 rue Scribe Paris

    r. Edited by David Ashley Inc. New York City

    s. Graveure originale de Louis Icart

Index

245